TWAYNE'S WORLD AUTHOR SERIES
A Survey of the World's Literature

Sylvia E. Bowman, Indiana University
GENERAL EDITOR

FRANCE

Maxwell A. Smith, Guerry Professor of French, Emeritus
The University of Chattanooga
Former Visiting Professor in Modern Languages
The Florida State University

EDITOR

Louis-Ferdinand Céline

TWAS 416

Photo Harlinque

Louis-Ferdinand Céline

LOUIS-FERDINAND CÉLINE

By DAVID O'CONNELL

University of Massachusetts, Amherst

TWAYNE PUBLISHERS

A DIVISION OF G. K. HALL & CO., BOSTON

Library of Congress Cataloging in Publication Data

O'Connell, David.
    Louis-Ferdinand Celine.

    (Twayne's world authors series ; TWAS 416 : France)
    Bibliography: p. 169 - 172
    Includes index.
    1. Destouches, Louis Ferdinand, 1894-1961. I Title.
PQ2607.E834Z795   843'.9'12 [B]   76-26059
ISBN 0-8057-6256-6

for David Tristan and Nathaniel Casey,
avid readers,
budding writers

Contents

About the Author

David O'Connell is Associate Professor of French at the University of Massachusetts, Amherst. He completed his Ph.D. at Princeton in 1966 where he was a National Woodrow Wilson Fellow, the Bergen Fellow in Romance Languages and a National Woodrow Wilson Dissertation Fellow. He completed his doctoral research in Paris as a Fulbright scholar. He is the author of *The Teachings of Saint Louis: A Critical Text* (North Carolina, 1972), *Les Propos de Saint Louis* (Gallimard, 1974) and the forthcoming *Instructions of Saint Louis: A Critical Text* to be published at North Carolina.

He has held research grants from the American Philosophical Society and the American Council of Learned Societies and his work has appeared, among other places, in the *Revue des Deux Mondes*, the *Revue des Lettres Modernes*, the *Revue d'Histoire Littéraire de la France*, the *French Review*, the *New York Times Book Review*, the *New Republic*, *Commonweal* and *America*.

Preface

This volume is intended as an introduction of Céline and his work to a literate, nonspecialist audience. On balance, perhaps as much space is devoted here to the man as to his writing, but given the deep autobiographical strain that runs through everything that Céline ever wrote, from *Voyage au bout de la nuit* to the posthumously published *Rigodon*, this task has proved to be inevitable. Also, given the fact that the mere mention of Céline's name can at times arouse passionate and nonrational reactions, and that, in the English-speaking world at least, his work and his thought are poorly understood outside of a small circle of specialists and enthusiasts, the time for a dispassionate, fair-minded, but hardly adoring book on Céline has now come. Unfortunately, in preparing this volume, we have discovered that in not a few instances American writers and reviewers have accused Céline of a variety of things that he cannot be proved to have done — such as marrying a prostitute or collaborating with the Gestapo during the war. We thus have attempted to set the record straight on precisely what was the nature of Céline's life, both private and political. For this reason we have devoted a whole chapter to his political pamphlets.

Another possible reason why Céline is not as well understood (and as widely read) as he ought to be by American audiences — especially since his influence is quite easily discernible in native writers like Henry Miller, Jack Kerouac, Kurt Vonnegut, Jr., Joseph Heller, William Burroughs, and Ken Kesey — is that his first, and in our opinion greatest, novel, *Voyage*, was poorly and inadequately translated forty years ago. The raw power of the sharp-edged prose of *Voyage* was dulled in large part because of the reigning censorship practices of those days. And then the novel's length, its density and its seemingly unremitting pessimism are probably also responsible for its often being unknown to those same American undergraduates who are nonetheless familiar with names like Gide, Malraux, Sartre, and Camus. It is hoped that before too long Céline's *Voyage* will be freshly translated.

Some *célinistes* will possibly disagree with our high assessment of *Voyage* in comparison to Céline's second novel, *Mort à crédit,* but we feel that *Voyage* is still Céline's most powerful book. It is perhaps slightly less stylistically audacious than *Mort,* but even though it does not use the "telegraphic" technique of the three dots as relentlessly, the same powerful poetic prose rhythms are still obvious and are coupled with a vision of life and of modern man's relationship to society that is the fountainhead from which flow many of the richest and most fertile streams of modernist and postmodernist literature.

We have also begun this volume with a chapter that is devoted solely to Céline's biography. This has been judged necessary since both he and his enemies have at times tried to distort, falsify, or suppress certain historical facts about his life. Thus, in order for a reader to have one sure place where he can find out exactly what we are sure did take place in Céline's life at a given time, we have included this chapter.

Céline is not easy for a foreigner to read in French. Luckily, with the exception of *Voyage,* the renderings of his later works in English have been in general very good to excellent. Thus, whenever possible we quote Céline in these usually quite readily available translations, giving the original French text in our notes. The closest thing we have to a complete critical edition of Céline's *oeuvre* is the five volume *Oeuvres de Louis-Ferdinand Céline,* published in Paris by Editions André Balland, 1966-69. These volumes do not include the three political pamphlets that Céline wrote after *Mea Culpa* and which we discuss at length below, because Céline, before he died, had his wife pledge to keep them out of print. He clearly wanted them to be forgotten. Fortunately, however, the Balland edition does bring together in one place virtually all of Céline's other work and accompanies it with excellent critical notes and commentaries. For this reason we quote from it here in our footnotes. At this time only *Voyage au bout de la nuit, Mort à crédit,* and the final trilogy *D'un château l'autre, Nord* and *Rigodon* are available in the prestigious Pléiade edition published by Gallimard, but it is rumored that the remaining Céline books will soon be added to these in the Pléiade collection.

Since this book is intended as an introduction to Céline that concentrates on the literary works, only passing attention is given here to his medical writings (with the exception of his doctoral thesis), his ballets, and other minor pieces. Once again, the curious reader is directed to the Balland edition of the *Oeuvres* for the texts and critical commentaries of this minor aspect of Céline's *oeuvre*. Finally, we have not treated here in all possible detail certain problems that we feel would be better handled in scholarly articles. Thus, we do not elaborate as completely as we could have on problems like the structure of *Voyage* and *Mort,* the relationship of *Casse-Pipe* to *Voyage*, and the other possible meanings that could be given to the "Légende du Roi Krogold" in *Mort à crédit*.

We have benefited during the preparation of this volume from the support of the Research Council of the University of Massachusetts, Amherst. Thanks also go to Ute Bargmann, Judith Schaefer, Marie Clark, William Markey, and, especially, Elizabeth Mahan of the library staff of the University of Massachusetts, Amherst. Their legwork has saved us many hours of labor and their constant patience and goodwill are deeply appreciated. Finally, thanks also go to Catherine Casey, to Olive Copeland, and to Frances Copeland who kindly consented to help with proofreading the manuscript.

Acknowledgment

I would like to express my gratitude to New Directions and to Delacorte Press for permission to quote Céline in English.

Chronology

1894   Louis-Ferdinand Destouches born in Courbevoie, just outside Paris. His father is a minor functionary in an insurance firm and his mother is a lacemaker.

1905   Awarded his *Certificat d'études*, after which he begins working as an apprentice and messenger boy in various trades.

1908 -   About this time spends a year each in Germany and England
1910   acquiring foreign languages.

1912   Begins a three year enlistment in the 12th Cavalry Regiment stationed in Rambouillet.

1914   Wounded in action near Ypres in October, is awarded the *médaille militaire* in November, and appears on the cover of the weekly *l'Illustré National* in December.

1915   His arm (not head) wounds are such that he is declared physically unfit for any more active duty. He is sent to London to work in the passport office there. While in London, is quietly married and divorced.

1916   Begins sojourn in the Cameroons with French lumber company; returns the following year.

1918   Works for the next three years for the Rockefeller Foundation in Brittany, dispensing information on tuberculosis, while continuing his secondary studies on his own in Rennes.

1919   Completes his *baccalauréat* and marries Edith Follet, daughter of the director of the medical school in Rennes.

1920   Birth of their daughter, Colette.

1924   Receives medical degree, writing doctoral thesis on Semmelweis.

1925 -   Leaves his family for good and under the aegis of the
1927   League of Nations travels to Switzerland, England, the Cameroons, Canada, the United States, and Cuba. Meets Elizabeth Craig.

1928   Sets up private practice in north end of Paris, specializing in obstetrics.

1931   Gives up private practice to work in a public dispensary.

1932   Publishes *Voyage au bout de la nuit* and is almost awarded the Goncourt Prize. Receives the Renaudot Prize instead.

1933   After more travels to Germany and England he publishes his only play, *L'Eglise*, written before *Voyage*.

1934   More travels to the United States.

1935   Meets Lucette Almanzor, whom he will marry in 1943.

1936   Publishes *Mort à crédit* and travels to the Soviet Union to spend royalties from Russian translation of *Voyage*.

1937   *Mea Culpa*, accompanied by thesis on Semmelweis, is published. *Bagatelles pour un massacre*, the first of three controversial pamphlets, appears including these ballets: *Naissance d'une fée, Voyou Paul brave Virginie* and *Van Bagaden*.

1938   The pamphlet *Ecole des cadavres* calls for a Franco-German alliance.

1939 -
1940   *Ecole des cadavres* withdrawn from circulation as a result of a lawsuit. Céline attempts to enlist in service; is refused and declared a seventy-percent invalid for his arm wound. Serves as ship's doctor, then in a clinic in Sartrouville, and finally in Bezons where he will remain until 1944.

1941   *Les Beaux draps*, his third pamphlet, appears.

1944 -
1945   Publishes *Guignol's Band I*, then leaves Paris after Allied landing and visits various German cities (accompanied by Lucette, their cat Bébert, and their friend Le Vigan) before escaping to Copenhagen, where he is imprisoned at the end of the war.

1947 -
1951   Released from prison but forbidden to leave Denmark, lives first in an attic in Copenhagen then in a hut near the Baltic. Answers attacks by Satre in a pamphlet, *A l'agité du bocal*. Written in 1948, it was privately published the following year. Publishes *Casse-Pipe* (1949) a fragment of a novel and two ballets *Foudres et fléches* (1949) and *Scandale aux abysses* (1950).

1951   Having been condemned to a year in prison and confiscation of half his possessions by a French court in 1950, he is amnestied in April and returns home in June.

1952   Signs a contract with Editions Gallimard for future works as well as for *Voyage, Mort, Guignol's Band I, Casse-Pipe, L'Eglise* and *Semmelweis*. Publishes *Féerie pour une autre fois I* and lives outside Paris in Meudon.

Chronology

1954   *Normance: Féerie pour une autre fois II* appears.

1955   *Entretiens avec le professeur Y* appears.

1957   *D'un château l'autre* is published. The five previously published ballets also appear together under title *Ballets sans musique, sans personne, sans rien.*

1960   *Nord* appears.

1961   Dies of a stroke on July 1. *Pont de Londres: Guignol's Band II,* will be published posthumously in 1964 as will *Rigodon* in 1969.

CHAPTER 1

The Voluntary Outsider:
Life as the Source of Art

I The Early Years

CÉLINE was born Louis-Ferdinand-Auguste Destouches on May 27, 1894. The grandson of a lycée professor in Le Havre, young Louis-Ferdinand was to grow up in somewhat less genteel surroundings than the ones enjoyed by his paternal grandfather.[1] His own father, Ferdinand-Auguste Destouches, was born in Le Havre in 1865, and he was able to complete his *baccalauréat* before marrying Marguerite-Louise-Céline Guilloux in 1893. The couple settled in Courbevoie, a Parisian suburb to the west of the city (past Neuilly and in the general direction of Nanterre) where, a year later in the spring of 1894, their son was born. Shortly after the birth of Louis-Ferdinand, the family moved to the passage Choiseul in the second *arrondissement,* one of the many narrow streets clustered to the east of the avenue de l'Opéra as it cuts its way in a northeasterly direction from the Palais-Royal to the place de l'Opéra. Here Louis-Ferdinand's mother ran a small lace shop[2] that enabled her to supplement the income earned by her husband, a white collar employe with an insurance company named *Le Phénix.*[3]

It was in this neighborhood that the youth grew up, attending first the local grade school, the *école communale,* located in the nearby square Louvois, and then completing his primary education and receiving his *Certificat d'études primaires* in the primary school in the rue d'Argenteuil located on the other side of the avenue de l'Opéra. Thanks to the vivid — although surely exaggerated — detail with which Céline describes these early years in *Mort à crédit* (1936), in particular the insalubrious living conditions in which he, his family, and neighbors existed in the passage

Choiseul, we can begin to understand the effect that this early social milieu must have had on this highly intelligent and gifted youngster who would grow to be the man who, in the eyes of many, would be nothing more than a warped misanthrope and a bigoted nihilist.

As an adolescent of about fourteen, Céline was dispatched to Germany by his parents in the hope that he would learn to speak German, a language his parents seem to have felt would be useful to him in the business world later on. He thus spent a year in Diepholz in Lower Saxony, and after completing this apprenticeship was sent off to England where he spent a year in a boarding school. But despite his intellectual abilities and an obvious gift for languages, he also lacked discipline during this period of his life. It seems that both in Germany and in England he became involved with women, in each case women who were both considerably older than he and married, and it is in this penchant for getting himself in trouble — indeed, in seeming to delight in trying to go out of his way to complicate his life — that we see the first adumbration in the character of the adolescent Louis-Ferdinand Destouches of the maverick personality of the later Céline.[4] Returning from England to Paris, he took up an assortment of positions in various business concerns over the next few years while preparing his *baccalauréat* on his own in his spare time. In 1912, a few months after successfully passing the first part of his *baccalauréat* exam, he seems to have reacted to one of his many arguments with his parents by signing on for a three year enlistment in the army, joining the *12e Régiment de Cuirassiers,* a cavalry unit based in nearby Rambouillet. Two years later, by the time war broke out, he had already risen to the rank of sergeant (*maréchal des logis*). Then on October 25, 1914, near Ypres, he was wounded in the arm, receiving a citation for heroic conduct under fire and, a month later, the prestigious *médaille militaire.* His exploits in combat were also commemorated on December 28 of the same year by the popular weekly, *L'Illustré National.* L.-F. Destouches, young war hero, was pictured on the cover that week.

During January 1915, an operation was performed on the young man's injured arm at the Paul Brousse Hospital in Villejuif on the outskirts of Paris. The "fracture du bras"[5] and the other damage done to his arm the previous October were tended to in this procedure which did not, in any way, deal with the patient's skull.

This point must be made forcefully at the outset, for in later years Céline was to claim that he had undergone trepanation at the hands of army surgeons in 1915. This claim, complicated as usual by the fact that the fictional Ferdinand Bardamu underwent trepanation, was a false one invented for reasons that grew out of Céline's desire to picture himself as an unjustly persecuted loner. In any case, we see established here, in the early years before L.-F. Destouches was to become the successful novelist Céline, a tendency to exaggerate suffering, to see a plot against him where there was none, to blame army doctors for chiselling away at his skull when in fact records of the operation tell us that only his arm was operated on. In March 1915, sergeant Destouches was sent off to London to work in the French passport office. Having just been granted convalescent leave for three months, he seems to have hurled himself into a whirlwind of activity once he arrived. Sharing a furnished room with a co-worker, he was able to devote the francs he saved on his rent to the pursuit of women, especially dancers and actresses, in the Soho district of London. The portrait of this period in Céline's life painted for us by Georges Geoffroy, who shared his lodgings with him, indicates that some other of those obsessions that would later characterize Céline the literary personality were already visible and prevalent in sergeant Destouches. His almost hysterical admiration for the ballet and for ballerinas, one of whom he seems to have married and divorced during this period, is symptomatic of these tendencies.[6]

Formally released from any further military obligation at the end of 1915, Destouches took a job as an agent with a French lumber company, the *Compagnie Forestière Sangho-Oubangui*, which was exploiting the occupied territory of the former German colony of the Cameroons. He remained there during a good part of 1916 until the spring of 1917 at which time he was sent back to France because of poor health. In addition to prolonged problems with his injured arm, a chronic case of enteritis made it necessary to dispatch him as quickly as possible to France.

Soon after his return to France, Destouches decided to move to Rennes, in Brittany, where he took a position for about the next three years with the Rockefeller Foundation. His duties there entailed quite simply making continuous circuit trips in the general area of Brittany lecturing and demonstrating to the local population the prophylaxis of tuberculosis. At the same time he

once again resumed his studies on his own, this time preparing for
his second *baccalauréat* which he would successfully complete in
July 1919 at the age of twenty-five. Thus, owing to the interruption
of military service and travel, he was already somewhat behind the
usual timetable for completion of secondary studies in France.

II   *Medicine and Literature*

We cannot say for sure how long Destouches had had his heart
set on practicing medicine, but by the time he completed his
secondary studies he clearly intended to pursue a career as a doctor.
In this regard, we can only guess at what connection there might
have been between this goal and the fact that in August 1919 he
married Edith Follet, the daughter of the director of the Rennes
Medical School. The following year, on June 16, their only child,
Colette, was born, and by June 1923 Destouches had completed his
studies at Rennes and obtained his medical degree. For the next two
years he practiced medicine while composing his doctoral thesis,
entitled *La Vie et l'oeuvre de Philippe-Ignace Semmelweis,* which
he completed in May 1924 and had published in Rennes the
following December.[7] In January 1925 he was awarded a bronze
medal by the medical faculty of the University of Paris for his
thesis, and shortly thereafter he seemed to be ready to settle down
into the solid mold of a bourgeois existence when he set up his own
office in Rennes. But here once again we find another of those
hallmarks of the later Céline — his tendency to reject others when
they offer themselves to him — for soon after settling down,
Destouches grew itchy to travel again. For this reason he went to
work late in 1925 as a doctor for the League of Nations and in so
doing turned his back on his wife and daughter for good. Thanks to
this new post, he would travel to Geneva and Liverpool, and even
back to the Cameroons briefly, before going on to the United
States, Cuba, and Canada. On this, his first trip to America, he
spent a good deal of his time in Detroit studying the social,
psychological, and medical problems of the Ford assembly line
workers there. During this period, around 1926, two other events
are also worthy of note: he wrote his only dramatic work, *L'Eglise*
(published 1933), and he seems to have begun his long association
with the American dancer Elizabeth Craig, to whom, a few years
later, in 1932, he would dedicate his first novel, *Voyage au bout de
la nuit.*

By 1928 Destouches had decided to return to Paris where he set up a private practice at 36, rue d'Alsace in a working class district on the right bank between the Gare de l'Est and the Gare du Nord. Living with him at this time was Elizabeth Craig who would remain at his side for the next four years or so until some time after the publication of *Voyage*. Working first at his private practice during the day, and then beginning in 1931 in a city health clinic, the *Dispensaire de Clichy,* located in a humdrum proletarian neighborhood, Céline devoted his free time from 1928 until 1932 to the composition of *Voyage.* Jeanne Carayon, his faithful secretary and neighbor in the rue d'Alsace, took care of typing and correcting his voluminous manuscript, and even after he closed his private practice and moved to Montmartre, where he took up residence at 98, rue Lepic in 1931, she continued to work for him. By the summer of 1932 the manuscript was ready for publication and Doctor Destouches sent it off to two different houses, Gallimard, growing at that time to become the reigning publishing house of the era (it already published Proust and Gide and would later gather under its wing Malraux, Sartre, and Camus), and to the new fledgling enterprise run by Denoël and Steele. This latter house had made its name with the publication in 1929 of Eugène Dabit's *Hôtel du Nord,* a novel that dealt with the same lower class stratum of society that Doctor Destouches worked with every day, and it is for this reason that the manuscript was also sent to them.[8]

According to Max Dorian, a young reader at Denoël and Steele, he was confronted one morning by a lady bearing a one thousand or so page manuscript which she claimed would be the literary event of the century if it could only be published. Showing Dorian a rejection letter from Gallimard which allegedly suggested that the author agree to publish the book at his own expense, this lady explained that she could not reveal the identity of the author, stating only that he wished to be known as "Céline" and was too impoverished to consider publishing the book himself. Dorian passed the text on to Robert Denoël, a young Belgian who, in cooperation with Bernard Steele, an American Jew, had boldly published several books, like *Hôtel du Nord,* over the past few years that no one else would touch. Denoël was said to have been so intrigued by the book that he called Dorian in the middle of the night to tell him that they should publish it. The next morning both Steele and Dorian read through the rest of the manuscript, but before they could sign a contract with their mysterious author, they first had to find him. After visiting the lady who had brought them the manuscript the day before, they were finally able to get her to send the unknown novelist back to their editorial offices in the rue Amélie. When he arrived, he sounded, to hear his speech, like a genuine Parisian proletarian, sprinkling his language with *argot* and exaggerating his pronunciation in that way so typical of lower class Parisians. Nonetheless, Denoël and Steele quickly concluded an agreement with Doctor Destouches before Gallimard, changing its mind, offered him a contract a few days later. Hoping naively that by publishing his novel under a pseudonym he could continue to practice medicine and thereby keep his two careers separate, Doctor Destouches discovered that just the opposite effect was about to take place for the simple reason that this other personage he had invented, the writer Céline, immediately attracted a great deal of attention. At this point, with his novel becoming a financial *succès de librairie* as well as a critical *succès d'estime*, he found himself becoming inundated by visits from curious readers of all kinds, from grateful proletarians who empathized with the bitter social protest dimension of the work to privileged literati who found in the language and *souffle* of the novel a passion for writing and a manipulation of the French language not seen since Rabelais.

Preparing the manuscript for publication was no small task. Jeanne Carayon, who had typed the work in its entirety and who knew the intricacies, techniques, and inner logic of Céline's prose like no one else, took over proofreading and editing of the novel after it went to press, for Céline himself would have nothing to do with it once it was accepted. The most intrepid of writers while still at work on a novel, forever correcting and rewriting his manuscript (and usually substantially augmenting the volume of the work in the process), he adamantly refused to correct it once it left his hands. For this reason the work of Jeanne Carayon is of the utmost importance, for it is she alone who was able in so many cases to preserve Céline's prose rhythms from the editors, first at Denoël and then later at Gallimard. The latter usually seem to have wanted to make it more limpid — that is, more classically French, Cartesian, and logical.

When the novel exploded on the literary landscape rather late in the year, in November of 1932, it was immediately hailed as a masterpiece and considered as a candidate for the prestigious

Goncourt Prize, an accolade that most novelists then and now covet because it assures a good deal of exposure and publicity, while also going a long way toward assuring a wide reading audience. Lucien Descaves,[9] one of the Goncourt Prize judges at the time, used his influence to see that the book received the prize, but at the last minute the judges, although strongly swayed by the influence of Descaves, nevertheless opted against Céline and gave the prize instead to a now unknown writer named Guy Mazeline, the author that year of the now long-forgotten novel *Les Loups*. Instead, Céline was awarded a kind of consulation prize in that the Théophraste Renaudot Prize was given to him.

This was small comfort, though, and the fact that a prize that most people agreed should rightfully be his was denied him at the last minute by what seemed to be backroom machinations could only help to contribute to the idea, now surely developing steadily in his mind, that one only sees the outer, exterior contour of events. Here, in the instance of the loss of this literary prize, and later in the events that were to lead to his dismissal from his position in the clinic where he was employed, as well as in those dark happenings that presaged the advent of World War II, Céline most likely felt that what was really going on was being kept from both him and the public by the press as well as by all those mysterious powers that wanted to maintain the status quo. As yet these dark powers were not specifically identified, being synonomous in his mind with the *bourgeoisie*, the class that he felt rules and exploits without giving any example worthy of emulation to those it takes advantage of. Only later would this brooding resentment find a more precise outlet in the pamphlets.

By December he seems to have been disillusioned by the Paris literary life. Leaving for Germany at the request of the League of Nations, he set out once more for a few months to study the effect that unemployment and its attendant social problems were having on the overall psychological health of the German people. While working in Breslau in early 1935, he renewed his friendship with a German girl, Erika Irrgang, whom he had first met in Paris early in 1932, but as usual he did not stay for long. In May 1933 we find him in London, but by June he is back on the continent, in Austria and in central Europe. He returned to Paris in October for the publication by Denoël and Steele of his play, *L'Eglise* (dedicated to the Danish ballerina Karen Marie Jensen), and by this time he was already at work on his second novel, *Mort à crédit*.

Early in 1934 Céline set out again in search of experience and sensation, spending most of the year, until August, in the United States. The reasons that seem to have led him to take this trip are most interesting and shed more light both on the character of Céline and on subsequent events in his life. Erika Ostrowsky has conjectured that his goal "was twofold: to search for Elizabeth Craig, who had returned to her country; [and] to arrange for a film version of *Voyage au bout de la nuit.*" [10] The search for Elizabeth Craig, about whose love affair with Céline we know very little except that it seems to have lasted from around 1926 until about 1932, was surely the primary motivation for the trip. Elizabeth had left without letting him know she was going, and the most Céline knew, or seems to have known, was that she was leaving him only temporarily in order to take legal action in the United States since her father had disinherited her. Unfortunately for Céline, she would wind up marrying the Jewish judge who presided at the hearing of her case and, in the words of Jeanne Carayon, "a Jewish judge took her away from him." [11] Céline's search was frantic, but nowhere was he able to find her. The loss was surely a profound one at the time, as the desperation of what we know of his search for her would seem to corroborate. [12]

The other reason that seems to have propelled him to go to the United States is also important, especially in light of the fact that in his later pamphlet, *L'Ecole des cadavres* (1938), he would rail against American movies, which by then (only four years later) he would see as manifestations of decadent Jewish culture. How interesting that he went so far in 1934 as to try to have his first novel turned into a movie in Hollywood.[13] But this only serves to illustrate one more complex aspect of Céline's character that would reveal itself over and over again in the future: that he hoped to get rich from his literary endeavors since he presumed that he could never amass a fortune by being a doctor. The idea of becoming rich by exploiting the physical misfortune of others repelled him. Thus he seems to have decided some time after he left his wife and child and the bourgeois comfort of a prestigious provincial medical practice in 1925 that he would henceforth practice medicine for the benefit of the poor without giving any thought to his own financial gain.

Returning to Paris, Céline seems to have had a succession of mistresses until he met Lucette Almanzor, a ballerina at Madame d'Alessandri's school. Recently returned from the United States, Lucette had been a wanderer of sorts herself. But little could she have expected at the time the changes of scene that the future would hold for her once she linked her life to Céline's. They became intimate and settled into life together; but one wonders, given the evidence that has come to light in recent years, about the true nature of their relationship. Up until the time Céline began to publish his novels, perhaps no serious literary writer had dealt as frankly and brutally with human sexuality as a purely animal function. Céline wantonly stripped sexual intercourse, and indeed all aspects of erotic interplay between man and woman, of their romantic aspects. To him it was all a simple question of biology. He also repeated over and over again in his work that what interested him in women was their beauty — but it was a beauty that one beholds, not that one clutches. Given this background, this is probably the best place to bring up the question of Céline's impotence. Admittedly a private matter, the question must nonetheless be discussed frankly here, for if in fact he was impotent, and there is a certain amount of evidence to make us suspect that he was, then this factor must be taken into consideration when analyzing both the man and his work.

Céline's old friend Marcel Brochard hints at impotence in recounting his memories of Céline and his mistress when he states that *Céline,* in dedicating *Voyage* to Elizabeth Craig, was also dedicating it to those other friends of his who often kept her company during the long evenings when he, Céline, did nothing but write his novel. Brochard also claims to have received a letter in which Céline hinted that impotence was upon him,[14] and this hint is corroborated by the statement, made by Céline to both Milton Hindus and to René Mahé,[15] that he preferred to have relationships with lesbian women because they were often beautiful and, even more importantly, they did not make sexual demands upon him. He wrote to Hindus, for example:

Free of all jealousy, Don Juanism, sadism, etc. ... I've never had enthusiasm for anything but the beauty of forms, fluidity, youth, grace, ... I'm very Athenian in that sense — But the literature on the subject? What boring merde! Health, vivacity, surprise, dance and every possible combination. In a word, I'm beastly! And, alas, I consume very little of it, concentrated as I am, on my huge workload. I'm so serious — in spite of myself — so scrupulous, ferocious in my work — I've always liked women to be beautiful and lésbian — Delightful to look at and leaving me absolutely alone with their sexual rantings. Let them enjoy themselves, play with each other, eat each other — me, I'm a voyeur, that's fine for me, just perfect, and it always has been! [16]

Of course, in this case, just as in the legend of the trepanation that Céline claimed to have undergone at the hands of army doctors in the early years of World War I, the critic must be on his guard. Céline wears many masks and often changes them both in real life and in his fiction, sometimes leading readers and critics astray in the process. Thus we cannot say for sure whether or not he was impotent and, if he was, we do not know when this condition began and how long it lasted. For the time being, then, it remains a mystery, but the possibility that he might have been troubled by impotence as early as his late thirties should be borne in mind for it can help us to understand his envy of and resentment toward Jews for their energy and activity in the worlds of medicine and the arts. Significantly, he would also later accuse Jews in the pamphlets of forever trying to seduce Gentile women. Thus, in the three areas that interested him the most, the worlds of medicine, of art, and of the erotic, he felt threatened. Perhaps considering himself impotent as a person, and of course seeing himself as an immunologist from a purely professional point of view, he saw all around him proliferating "parasites" that would soon be conveniently labelled as "Jews."

Living with Lucette, Céline continued working on his second novel. *Mort à crédit* appeared in July 1936 and it confirmed for many critics that Céline was indeed a genius, while others were appalled at the unmitigated blackness and seemingly absolute nihilism of the author. By this time Jeanne Carayon had married, leaving Céline to go to America with her new husband. Céline's remark in this instance is not surprising. Commenting on her marriage, an institution from which he himself had fled, abandoning his wife, child, and comfortable career in the process, he is said to have stated: "An honest woman doesn't change names...." [17] But luckily for him Jeanne was soon replaced by another dedicated and capable secretary, Marie Carnavaggia, who would edit and type all his future manuscripts.

Mort à crédit, which like *Voyage* is autobiographical in inspiration, treats Ferdinand Bardamu's childhood and culminates at the end of adolescence where *Voyage* had begun. When we say Bardamu's childhood and not Céline's, it is to reaffirm once again the necessity of keeping the two worlds separate. This is not to deny that Bardamu owes a lot to Céline and indeed has much in common with him. This is, of course, true. But the transformation of Céline's life that we find in these first two novels is so drastic — especially in *Mort* where the portrait of his parents is so terribly distorted against them — that the distinction must continually be made so as not to fall into the trap of mistaking one for the other.

III   *The Pamphleteer*

In the summer of 1936, Céline was invited to travel to the Soviet Union. Since the Soviets would not transfer out of that country the royalties that had accrued to him as a result of the Russian translation of *Voyage* by Aragon and Elsa Triolet, he would have to go there to spend the money. He spent a good part of August and September in Russia and was sickened by the police state he saw there. Having been courted by important critics on the French left who had found the criticism of bourgeois society made in *Voyage* much to their liking, he was more or less considered by leftist intellectuals to be Socialist and Communist or at least left wing in sympathy, and thus the trip was looked upon both in France and in Russia as a possible propaganda coup of considerable importance.

That same summer another group of intellectuals, led by Gide, was also going to Russia under the aegis of the *Association des Ecrivains Anti-Fascistes et Révolutionnaires*, but, unlike the members of this group, for whom the bills were paid by the Soviets, Céline went on his own and paid his own way.[18] When he came back he would write a pamphlet about his experience that would disassociate him for good from the leftist parties in France and turn him into an avowed enemy of all Communists. The pamphlet, *Mea Culpa*, would be published the following year. Of course, the Soviets knew that the celebrated author would write a book about his trip and they presumed that it would be laudatory. Céline's friend Gen Paul has intimated that the Russians went out of their way to court Céline while he was writing the book, even going so far as to send one of their diplomats to his house to remind him of the profits a warmly pro-Soviet book would reap for him in Russia once it was translated and sold there. But Céline had other ideas in mind: as Gen Paul (who witnessed Céline's meeting with the Russian diplomat Braun), puts it: "I was highly amused, knowing that Céline, a delicate and honest man, without needs, without vices, without a car, without a servant, a nonsmoker who drank only water, was one of those very rare beings who couldn't be had. A man who couldn't be bought."[19]

In December of 1936, *L'Eglise*, which no Parisian producer would touch, was finally staged by a group of amateurs in Lyons. It played for only one night and then died, for Céline as a dramatist does not pack the same punch that he does as a novelist. The play has been produced only once since,[20] and it can in no way be considered as an important work. In fact, it would be of virtually no interest except for the fact that it is Céline who wrote it. When *Mea Culpa* came out in 1937, Céline agreed to add to it his doctoral thesis which was now published under the name of Céline and not under that of Destouches. It seems that one of the reasons for republishing this work at the time was to attentuate somewhat Céline's monstrous image by showing that, in the case of Semmelweis at least, he had been able to feel some compassion for another human being.

Not long after this, Céline got to work on what was to be his next novel, *Casse-Pipe* (*Kick the Bucket*), which was to deal in depth with his wartime experiences. But he interrupted the work in order to compose two "pamphlets," *Bagatelles pour un massacre* (*Trifles for a Massacre*, 1937) and *Ecole des cadavres* (*School for Cadavers*, 1938), both of which attacked those segments of the French population that were calling for war, notably the Jews. A whole chapter in the present volume is devoted to these so-called "pamphlets," which are in fact lengthy, disorganized, and boringly repetitive diatribes against Jews, freemasons, the English, the Catholic Church, the average Frenchman, and most French politicians, especially Léon Blum and his cohorts in the Popular Front Government (1936-38). In the second of these pamphlets, Céline even goes so far as to call for a Franco-German alliance — a fact that indicates that the man who was independent enough to criticize the Soviet Union in 1936 when many had expected him to do just the opposite continued to display his independence in 1938, for at that time even the most fanatical of French fascists could not openly call for a Franco-German alliance. This trait — the desire to preserve complete and total independence from any political, social, or aesthetic group or *chapelle* of any kind — is also surely one of the prime traits of Céline's character. In fact it is this independence of mind that would involve him in so much trouble in later years.

But this refusal to conform to most accepted standards of conduct was also unfortunately complicated in his case by the fact that things also seem to have just happened to him. Just as he had undergone the horrible experience of 1914 when he was seriously wounded and decorated for bravery, so unusual events would continue to crop up in his life. The trip to the Isle of Jersey with Lucette in May of 1937 is a case in point. For some reason or other, the British government presumed that the author of *Voyage* was an enemy of the crown. Thus, shortly after Céline's arrival on Jersey, to which he had fled (the notion of fleeing, of running away is a permanent way of seeing reality — or of escaping from it — for Céline) in the hope of getting some rest and a change from the turbulent events taking place in Paris, he was systematically harassed by British authorities. "In view of the coronation and the influx of visiting dignitaries to London, the British police had taken exceptional precautions. As a result several incidents occurred. ... Louis-Ferdinand Céline, author of *Voyage au bout de la nuit*, was suspected of wishing to assassinate George VI and put under surveillance on the Isle of Jersey. His passport was confiscated. Despite the protests of the French Consul, the British police insisted on continuing to search the island for Céline's 'accomplices.' [21] Needless to say, the British intelligence service would be attacked ferociously in both *Bagatelles* and *Ecole*. This freakish incident could not help but have an effect on a man who already had a tendency to see plots where in fact there were none.

When Céline returned from Jersey in June he gave up his apartment in the rue Lepic in Montmartre where he had lived since 1931, probably moving to a hotel for a while. Later that year, in December, two important events were to take place in his life. First, *Bagatelles* was published, irrevocably putting Céline in the fascist camp as a Germanophile (which deep down inside he really was not), an Anglophobe, and an anti-Semite (both of which he was). The second major event that took place during this month was that Céline was forced to resign from his position at the *Dispensaire de Clichy* where he had worked for over six years. It is alleged that he was forced out of his job by a Jewish refugee doctor from

Lithuania, an allegation which, if true, might have some bearing on Céline's hatred of Jews.[22]

In November 1938 *Ecole des cadavres* appeared, separating Céline from the fascist supporters who had welcomed *Bagatelles*,[23] and then the following year saw the outbreak of the war that Céline had dreaded so much. In June 1939, just before the invasion of Poland by Germany and Russia, *Ecole* was withdrawn from publication as a result of a lawsuit brought against the book, but once hostilities began, the maverick individual who had railed against this war (which he had clearly seen coming, and which he blamed on the machinations of the Jewish war party in France, England, and the United States), did not hesitate to enlist in the service of his country. Céline's attempt to enlist for the duration of the war was denied however for medical reasons. As the "phony war" held France in its sway all through the end of 1939, Céline tried to set up a new private practice in Saint-Germain-en-Laye, but this attempt at a fresh start ended in failure. In November, however, the French government did finally get around to recognizing that as a result of the war injuries he had suffered in 1914, he could be declared a seventy-percent invalid with a pension that corresponded to such a disability. This was the first time that Céline was ever to benefit from French government social services in any way, for all through the years he had worked at the *Dispensaire de Clichy* it seems that he had never been assigned to the type of position that led to a paid vacation, a pension, and other extra benefits.

As usual with Céline, when frustrated he would take flight. Thus, over the winter he found employment as a ship's doctor on an armed passenger ship, the *Shella*, which made periodic trips back and forth between Marseille and Casablanca. But when the ship was seriously damaged near Gibralter in early 1940 in a naval encounter with a British patrol boat, it was destroyed by the Germans after limping back to port at Marseille. The phony war continued through the winter and into the next year and during this time Céline, still frustrated at not being able to take part against the Germans with whom he had only recently called for a military alliance, found a new post in Sartrouville, a grim Parisian suburb, as a replacement for a French doctor called up for active service.

When the real outbreak of hostilities came in the summer of 1940, Céline drove from Paris to La Rochelle in the west of France in the ambulance from the dispensary where he was employed. Lucette, along with an eighty year old woman and two babies, were with him on the trip as he tried to escape to the west before the advancing Germany army. He remained in La Rochelle for two weeks caring for the injured and infirm and then became the doctor at a worker camp nearby at Saint-Jean d'Angély.

By October he was back in Paris at his mother's apartment (his father had been dead since 1932), where he had lived intermittently since leaving his apartment in the rue Lepic in 1937. But shortly thereafter he found an apartment for himself in Montmartre just opposite the *Moulin de la Galette* nightclub, and also took a position as head of a dispensary in suburban Bezons. The address of his house was 4, rue Girardon, an address that during the ensuing years would be important to the Résistance fighters who often met there in the apartment just underneath Céline's. Here once again we find one of those seeming contradictions in Céline's character which, on further examination, turns out to be just another manifestation of his unusually strong spirit of independence. This is so because the same man who was at work during 1940 and 1941 writing his last pamphlet on contemporary political affaires, *Les Beaux draps* (*A Nice Mess*, 1941), and who also received important French fascists like Lucien Rebatet as his guest, also knew about the clandestine meetings that were taking place underneath him. Céline even went so far as to give medical care to an injured *résistant* who was brought to him by Robert Champfleury, the owner of the downstairs apartment, and never in all those years did he reveal to the Nazis that meetings were being held there.[24]

This point must be made forcefully and clearly, for it is sometimes written that Céline was a "collaborator" and that he did the work of the Nazis against his fellow Frenchmen. This is simply untrue. Céline did not "collaborate," although he did carry on a personal relationship with Karl Epting, the director of the German Institute in Paris during the war, and accepted an invitation to visit, in the company of a group of French doctors, hospitals in Berlin in 1942. At the same time, thanks to Lucien Rebatet, editor of the French fascist weekly *Je Suis Partout*, we know that Céline had sent several articles to that magazine in the hope that they would be published. But the reason they did not get into print was that they were so strongly and vehemently racist in tone that even the French henchmen of the Nazis could not print them. Thus we have here not a collaborator, but an eccentric, albeit a vengeful and racist one.

On the other hand, Rebatet has recounted for us his recollection of the initial meeting of a front organization the Nazis had created in Paris and to which they had given the name *Institut des Questions Juives*. At its initial meeting a French Jew-hater read a speech in which he was in the midst of attaching "la tyrannie judéo-marxiste," when Céline shouted from the audience: "Hey, how about Aryan baloney, won't you talk about that?" The room was thrown into a frenzy, a fistfight ensued between Céline and a German soldier, and the meeting ended shortly thereafter with everyone in a state of confusion. Céline, who was already receiving through the mail little wooden caskets sent to him by the Résistance (as a reminder that he had been singled out by them for assassination), and who had already had his death sentence read out over radio London, was here engaged in an action that, if undertaken by anyone else, would have been considered the act of a pro-Jewish fanatic.[25]

But what is perhaps even more enigmatic about this contradictory conduct is the fact that Céline seems to have been convinced as early as the fall of 1940, when Germany's fortunes were at their heights, that the verdict was already in — for to his mind Germany had already lost the war. When he made this statement to Lucien Rebatet (at the time, we recall, he was writing *Les Beaux Draps*), he was asked why he could believe such a thing. After all, the Americans were not in the war yet (and Hitler was doing his utmost to keep them out), and the Germans still seemed capable of defeating everyone else on the continent. But, independent-minded creature that he was, Céline responded: "The Germans are finished, and us with them. An army that doesn't bring a revolution along with it in a war like this one is cooked. The Krauts are done for."[26]

In the midst of all these turbulent events, Céline and Lucette, perhaps suspecting that the end was near, decided to get married. They were wed in a civil ceremony in February 1943 and continued to live in the rue Girardon until the Allied landing took place in Normandy in June 1944. But while waiting for what he took to be the inevitable outcome of the conflict, Céline continued to write. In addition to republishing in 1943 *Ecole des cadavres*, which had been withdrawn from circulation in 1939, he also published, in

April 1944, a new novel entitled *Guignol's Band*. This fictional work, which, like the first two, is largely autobiographical in inspiration, is set in London during World War I, and brings together an assembly of underworld characters of unsavory background and comportment. The innovative style first fully demonstrated in *Mort* — that is, the short bits of sentences separated by Céline's three dots, like short bursts of machine gun fire — was confirmed as the hallmark of his work here. The style he was moving toward in *Voyage*, one designed to be read aloud so as to give full expression to his rhythmic prose, had finally been born with *Mort*, and then confirmed with the publication of *Guignol's Band*.

IV   *Flight from the Allies*

When Céline fled from Paris in July 1944 a whole new journey was about to begin. Accompanied by his friend the movie actor Le Vigan, as well as by Lucette and their cat Bébert, Céline's new *voyage* would be the inspiration for most of his later work. The reason for his flight should be obvious enough. He felt that if he remained in Paris until it was liberated from German occupation, he would be summarily executed by his political enemies. Rather than face such a fate, he decided that the time had come to attempt to lay hold of the cache of gold he had put aside in Denmark during the thirties, years before the war had even begun. Having been convinced at that time that a new war was inevitable, and attributing a very special importance to the money he had earned with his writing, he had taken his savings and sent them to Denmark where they were said to have been buried in the garden of his friend, the Danish ballerina Karen Marie Jensen, to whom he had dedicated *L'Eglise*.[27]

The probable reasons for his sending this money to Denmark are that (1) he did have a friend there in Karen Jensen and (2) he probably expected that Denmark's neutrality would be respected in the next war just as it had been during World War I. His plan when he left Paris was to move as rapidly as possible across the crumbling *Reich* to claim his fortune in Copenhagen before it was too late.

If we can believe Céline's recounting of the effect that the attempted assassination of Hitler (July 20, 1944) had on the various characters living in Baden-Baden at that time, then he had already arrived there from Paris and taken up residence. Baden-Baden, located just inside the German border and not far from Strasbourg, is the site of a spa. Until the aborted assassination of the *Reichsführer,* it had welcomed wealthy aristocrats, industrialists, widows of high ranking officers of the *Wehrmacht,* and other members of Germany's privileged classes, for these people knew that in addition to the healing waters to be found there, they could also procure excellent wines and culinary delights that were difficult to get hold of elsewhere in the *Reich.* Céline's sojourn in the Park Hotel there could not have lasted very long, for we know that shortly after the July 20 incident word was sent from Berlin to disperse the residents of the resort since it was suspected that they might have wanted to see Hitler dead. Thus, before long, Céline and his small entourage were sent north to Berlin where they spent about two weeks in an already ruined city trying to obtain exit visas. Exasperated by the fruitlessness of his search, Céline finally made contact with a German doctor serving in the SS, Dr. Harras, whom he had met a few years before in Paris. This medical colleague, a francophile and an admirer of Céline, used his influence to get him out of Berlin and had him sent still farther north to Zornhof, a small village near Neuruppin, about forty miles from Berlin.[28] Céline has recounted in *Nord* — of course in transposed fashion — the life they led at Zornhof among the various kinds of displaced persons that the administrators and bureaucrats of the crumbling *Reich* had assembled there. Needless to say, situated so close to the Danish border, Céline did all he could to get across, but was unable to get beyond Warnemünde on the Baltic. His refusal to make radio broadcasts for the Nazis also did not help him any at this time.

By autumn it was becoming obvious that Céline and his companions were not about to obtain the visas they so desperately sought. Instead, word came to them that they were to be sent south to Sigmaringen in the Black Forest where, since September 8, 1944, Pétain had been residing in the seventh floor apartment of the Hohenzollern Castle. Shortly after Pétain's arrival, Laval and other personalities from the Vichy government arrived in their turn to take up what was hoped at the time would be only a temporary residence while Germany prepared its new counteroffensive and continued work on the new, mysterious secret weapon that would enable the *Reich* to avoid total surrender. Robert Aron, in his

Histoire de Vichy, has divided this sojourn of French collaborators in Germany into three periods: the period of installation, the period of hope, and, finally, that of panic and collapse. Céline, who arrived in November and would leave before the others, would witness only the second of these three time periods.[29] Officially assigned as resident doctor to the French colony of more than one thousand persons, he would initially see his patients in his hotel room at the Hotel Löwen, and only later assume the offices of a German doctor who had been called elsewhere. Although the French flag floated from the rooftop of the castle, and despite the fact that the fleeing Frenchmen all shared to some degree the aspirations and beliefs of Germany's National Socialists, they were still despised by the local townsfolk. The latter, predominantly anti-Nazi and angry that their prince had been evicted from his home to make room for the French, were also angry that the peace and security that their town had enjoyed until then now risked being seriously compromised.

Céline has been likened to a migrating bird who foresees the change in the weather and is the first to fly off. The comparison artfully describes his flight from Sigmaringen in early March 1945, for Céline, the first to sniff out the imminent catastrophe, escaped from that condemned heap of humanity a full month before the others began to flee in April. His own flight across Germany must have been a nightmare for, with the trio of Le Vigan, Lucette, and Bébert, he completed the trip on one of the last trains to get through to the Danish border before the line was cut. Arriving in Copenhagen on March 27, 1945, they went straight to Karen Marie Jensen's apartment where they took up residence. We are not sure, as noted above, exactly where Céline's fortune was located, but he must have learned shortly after his arrival in the Danish capital that his money would not be recovered. To this day, no one seems to know what happened to it. It was here too that he would learn of the death of his mother, who had passed away the preceding March 6.

On April 19, a French court issued a warrant for Céline's arrest but it was only eight months later, on December 18, after France had been completely liberated, that the attaché of the French Legation in Copenhagen, demanded Céline's immediate arrest and extradition. On Christmas Eve 1945, both Lucette and Louis-Ferdinand were taken by Danish authorities and put into prison,[30] she for two and a half months and he for fourteen. Once Lucette was set free she was able to support herself by giving ballet lessons, but even then she was only allowed to see her husband (who was stuck away in a cell on death row to await extradition) for ten minutes each week during which time they had to speak English to each other in the presence of two prison guards. By February 1947, the Danish government had still refused to extradite Céline, whose health was steadily failing. A poor diet had caused him both to lose weight and to come down with pellagra, a chronic disease caused by niacin deficiency and characterized by skin eruptions, digestive and nervous disturbances, and eventual mental deterioration. The Danish minister of justice then intervened in the case and had him sent to a hospital where he remained off and on until June of that year, at which time he was set free after having given his word in writing that he would not leave Denmark without the permission of Danish authorities.[31]

At first the only place they had to go was to the attic in Copenhagen's Kronprinssessegade where Lucette had been giving her ballet lessons. But shortly thereafter, Céline's attorney, Thorwald Mikkelson, lent them a cottage at his property, Klarskovgaard, on the Baltic near Körsor. They would remain there from the autumn of 1947 until his amnesty was granted in April 1951. In the meantime he would work on *Féerie pour une autre fois* (*Fairy-tale for Another Time*, 1952), and on *Normance: Féerie pour une autre fois II* (1954), and engage in a voluminous correspondence. When accused by Sartre in *Les Temps Modernes* of having been paid by the Nazis to collaborate,[32] his letter of protest to a French paper was not printed. But his pamphlet, *A l'agité du bocal* (*To the Fretful Man in the Glass Jar*), an *ad hominem* diatribe addressed to Sartre, was printed privately by friends the following year. What made matters worse, financially at least, was that after the mysterious assassination of Robert Denoël in 1945, Céline was essentially a writer without a publisher. Publication of *Casse-Pipe* (*Kick the Bucket*), part of a novel dealing with Bardamu's experiences in 1914, by P. Chambriand in 1949; of a ballet, *Scandale aux Abysses* (*Scandal in the Depths*), in 1950 by the same publisher; and of the ballet *Foudres et fléches* (*Sparks and Arrows*) in 1949 by Ch. de Jonquiéres received hardly any critical notice when they appeared. This was so probably as much because Céline was being unofficially ignored in literary circles as because he did not have the weight of an important publishing house behind him.

In all honesty, though, there is not much compelling artistic value in his work during this period. It was quite easy to ignore.

V   *Twilight in Meudon*

When the publishing house of Denoël was exonerated in April 1947 of any guilt of collaboration with the enemy, this appeared to be a good sign to those who supported repatriation and acquittal of Céline. This house, which had published *Bagatelles pour un massacre* and *Ecole des cadavres* before the war, and then *Les Beaux draps* and *Ecole* again during the war, was found not guilty of the following accusatory question: "The Denoël Publishing Company, a moral entity, was it guilty, in Paris, between 16 June 1940 and the date of Liberation, of having printed and published brochures and books favoring the enemy, of collaboration with the enemy, of racism, and of totalitarian doctrines?"[33] Céline, buoyed by this decision, kept writing letters on his own behalf to those who showed him sympathy. Among these were Albert Paraz and a doctor Camus in France, the Swedes Ernzt Bendz and Ole Nordling, and the American Milton Hindus.[34]

Céline's case finally came to trial in February 1950. Although he was not present, he was represented by counsel and had also taken the liberty of writing many letters in his own defense directly to the judge.[35] The accusations brought against Céline were contained in the two following questions:

First question: Is Destouches, Louis-Ferdinand, also known as Louis-Ferdinand Céline, accused but not present, guilty of having knowingly committed, in France, between 1940 and 1944, in any case between 16 June 1940 and the date of Liberation, in time of war, acts of a kind detrimental to National Defense?

Second question: Was the action specified above under Question One committed with the intention of furthering any of the designs of Germany, an enemy power of France, or of any of the other Axis powers at war against the Allied nations?[36]

Although the verdict returned by the jury was not unanimous, a majority of the jurors did find him guilty on both counts. He was therefore condemned to a year of prison, a fine of 50,000 francs, confiscation of his goods, and perpetual disgrace. By this time, of course, Céline had already spent over a year in prison and had been an almost perpetual outcast since the late thirties. As for his possessions, which were to be confiscated, there was nothing more to take. When he fled from Paris in July 1944, he had been imprudent enough to leave several manuscripts behind in his apartment in the rue Girardon. They, with all his other possessions, were ruthlessly pillaged later on. Thus, virtually penniless, and living in a shack where he depended to a large extent on charity for his very survival, Céline found himself the recipient of a formalized legal punishment that in fact he had already been suffering for some time.

Needless to say, many people in the press were hostile to the verdict. The most indignant reactions predictably came from the left, and as usual did not hesitate to lie about Céline. The Communist daily *L'Humanité* lamented that Céline, as an "agent de la Gestapo," had been let off all too easily, while Madeleine Jacob, writing in *Liberation*, was upset that an "alcoolique" like Céline (we recall that he neither drank nor smoked) should receive such clemency.[37] A year later, in April 1951, Céline received an amnesty which granted him permission to return home free of fear of legal action. By June he was in France, first spending a month in the south, in Menton, with Lucette's mother, then coming north to Paris where they lived with friends while looking for a place of their own. On August 18, 1951, Gallimard bought the rights to *Voyage*, *Mort*, *Guignol's Band I*, and *Casse-Pipe*, and also contracted to publish all his future work. Taking up residence outside Paris in the small town of Meudon where Dr. Destouches put out his shingle to lure would-be patients (while Lucette began once again to earn a living by giving dancing lessons), they finally resumed, after years of hardship, a somewhat normal existence. Encouraged by a contract and financial support from Gallimard, Céline published *Casse-Pipe* (1962), *Féerie pour une autre fois* (1952), and its sequal *Normance* (1954) in rapid succession.

The first of these was probably written by Céline in the late thirties and recounts some of Bardamu's adventures before he was wounded, while the two latter volumes are set in Paris during the Occupation and blend the usual biographical material (transposed by the author), with delirium scenes that seem to leap out of Céline's pen and assault the reader. The famous fantastic scene of the bombardment of Montmartre in *Féerie,* wholly imagined, is perhaps the prime example of delirious writing in these works. The following year, *Entretiens avec le professeur Y (Conversations with Professor Y)* appeared, in which Céline propounded in his usual mock-serious style the basic principles of his *ars poetica.* Unfortunately, none of these books attracted much serious critical attention and in fact it is difficult to say that they deserved any. The silence and critical indifference that often follow the death of a major author appeared to be taking place while Céline was still alive and writing. Many critics seem to have decided that Céline was finished, that he had nothing new to say, and that the inspiration that had driven him to write *Voyage* and *Mort* was beyond resurrection. He was being forgotten.

Boldly, however, Roger Nimier cried out against this tendency and called for a Nobel Prize for Céline.[38] This quixotic gesture was not taken very seriously by many people but at least it testified to the fact that even at the lowest ebb of Céline's literary fortunes, when most people thought his career was over (when indeed they thought of him at all), there were those who still recognized his particular genius. Finally, in 1957, critical attention was attracted to the forgotten doctor of Meudon by the publication of *D'un château l'autre (Castle to Castle).* This book, like *Voyage,* is a tale of flight, dealing among other things with life at Sigmaringen in 1944-45. With a few minor exceptions, critics were at least civil to Céline no matter what they thought of his new book. When *Nord (North)* appeared in 1960, the same critical tendencies were evident once again. In this book, just as he had backtracked in *Mort,* telling in that book of events in Bardamu's life that had taken place before those described in *Voyage,* Céline also told of his own adventures in Baden-Baden, Berlin, and Zornhof, episodes of the year 1944 that had taken place before his assignment to Sigmaringen. Outright *ad hominem* thrusts against him were less in evidence by this time so that criticism could finally be addressed to the work itself.

All this time Céline and Lucette lived a hermetic existence, seeing only a few friends and surrounding themselves with a houseful of pets, their only steady companions. Still suffering from headaches, the intermittent buzzing sound in his ears, and from a partially paralyzed right arm and hand, results of the wounds received in 1914, Céline also continued to be a victim of that chronic insomnia that had haunted his whole adult existence and he might also have been, as we mentioned above, impotent. In this state, he seems to have devoted virtually all of his waking hours to his writing. Right up until the day he died on July 1, 1961, he kept at it, putting the finishing touches on *Rigodon* (*Rigadoon,* 1969), a sequel to *Castle to Castle* and *North* that concentrates on the final stages of his flight to Scandinavian exile. All three books are also attempts at political self-justification. When his death came as a result of a cerebral stroke, his work was not finished and several of his manuscripts had not been prepared for publication. Among these was the text of the sequel to *Guignol's Band,* which was published under the title of *Pont de Londres: Guignol's Band II.* Like the former work, it followed the partially veiled adventures of Céline, transposed as Bardamu, in London during World War I. The only other work published by Céline during these Meudon years was the collection of ballets entitled *Ballets sans musique, sans personne, sans rien* (*Ballets Without Music, Without Anybody, Without Anything,* 1959), but this work was hardly original for most of the descriptions for ballets had already been published in *Bagatelles.*

Lucette gave notice of Céline's death to only a few close friends. About thirty people are said to have witnessed his burial on the morning of July 4, 1961, and it was only the next morning that the media flashed the news to the public. He had been buried in the public cemetery of Bas-Meudon, and on his grave a simple stone would soon be marked with the inscription:

Louis-Ferdinand Céline

Le Docteur Destouches

1894-1961

His wish had been that his remains be tossed in a common grave but Lucette spared him this last ignominy just as, in keeping his death a secret until after his burial, she had assured his passing a dignity that the press and certain enemies among the public would most likely not have otherwise accorded him. She also planted a holly bush at his gravesite as if, in honor of those Celtic origins that Céline boasted of so often ("a Celt in every inch of my miserable body"),[39] this last pagan gesture would mark the return to nothing of a Celtic bard. The *Voyage au bout de la nuit* had ended.

CHAPTER 2

A Great Beginning

I Genesis and Publication of Voyage

WHEN *Voyage au bout de la nuit* burst on the literary horizon, most critics had to agree, no matter what their preconceived notions about what a novel should be like and what kind of language it should use, that a new star had been born in the French literary firmament. This book, one of the greatest novels in French literature and, in our opinion, the work on which Céline's reputation will largely rest in future years, found its way into print in a rather interesting manner.

Max Dorian, reader of manuscripts at Denoël and Steele publishers, was at work one morning when Céline's secretary at the time, Jeanne Carayon, brought a package containing a thousand or so typed pages into his office and asked to talk to Mr. Denoël himself. She was quite upset when told that he was unavailable at the moment for, as she assured Dorian, once this book was published, it would be the "literary event of the century." [1]

On Céline's order, she refused to divulge the real identity of the author so that the next day (after Bernard Denoël had spent the night reading the manuscript and then waited the whole morning while Dorian and Steele read it), when it came time to contact the author to sign a contract with him, they could only get to him through his secretary who agreed that she would pass the message along to him. It is in this way that the three readers of *Voyage* in manuscript form finally got a glimpse of the cryptic novelist who from the beginning seemed to be doing what he could to conceal his true identity. But why did the doctor from Clichy feel compelled to take on one of his mother's given names as a pseudonym? The reason given from the very beginning by Céline for this adoption of a literary name is that he hoped in doing so to remain anonymous, to separate his two existences so that he could go on practicing medicine under one name while collecting substantial literary royalties under the other. Populism was in the air, and Eugène Dabit, he thought, had gotten rich from writing *Hôtel du Nord*, so why could he not do the same thing? "At that time the populists, like Dabit whom I knew a bit, were in style ... shot in the dark! ... 1932 ... I took my mother's given name, Céline, so no one would spot me. ..."[2]

The novel appeared rather late in 1932, but despite this fact it was warmly greeted by critics of varying persuasions.[3] Léon Daudet, a member of the Goncourt jury and a critic with the royalist newspaper *Action Francaise,* hailed the book as a masterpiece. When it came time for voting, however, the members of the jury were frightened by the prospect of awarding the prize, which theoretically assures a widely based rate of sale, to a book which made such liberal use of slang, obscenities, and vulgarities, and which painted such a bleak picture of the human condition. They thus gave the prize to Guy Mazeline, author of the now long-forgotten novel *Les Loups*, and, in place of the Goncourt, which he would have liked to receive, Céline was later awarded the Prix Renaudot as a kind of consolation prize. Deeply offended at the rejection of the man they had supported, both Daudet and Lucien Descaves[4] stormed out of the Goncourt meeting in protest. The inevitable cause célèbre followed and Céline, who had already given indications of feeling estranged from a society whose values he almost completely rejected, could secretly at first, and then outwardly, rejoice in having been rejected by the literary establishment.

Céline himself has stated on several occasions that the reason he decided to become a writer was in order to earn money. One would ordinarily be tempted to dismiss this avowal of entering the literary world in order to acquire wealth, since we know that he had already begun to keep a notebook while still a soldier in 1914.[5] In other words, the impulse to write, to write something — anything — if not necessarily novels about life in the working class districts of Paris, seems to have existed in him at a fairly early date. Added to this is the fact that he started working on *Voyage* around 1928, devoting a good deal of his free time to it, and, according to one observer, seemed to be chained to his desk evenings in order to write his novel. This evidence that Céline was in fact writing because he was following the direction of an inner logic, a compulsive desire to say what he felt he had to communicate, does not sit too well with his later comment that he wrote *Voyage* because he wanted to "earn a little money to pay my rent." He goes on: "That guy Eugène Dabit had made lots of money with *Hôtel du Nord,* which he stuffed with his childhood memories. So I said to myself: 'I can do that too. Let's go!'" [6]

Obviously, it could not have been as simple as all that and this comment by Céline is typical of the kind of trail the critic must follow in dealing with the man and his work. He surely had sent his manuscript to Denoël and Steele precisely because they had published *Hôtel du Nord* and for that reason he might have thought that they would be disposed to giving his work a sympathetic reading. They had made money with that work, published in 1929, and were probably on the lookout for something along the same lines. If indeed this was what Céline had in mind when he sent them his manuscript we surely cannot hold it against him, for writers, especially novice ones, must obviously give thought to these kinds of questions before they send off their work. But we cannot go any further than this. And when Céline tells us that he wrote the book in order to supplement his income, his statement cannot be rejected out of hand for we have to bear in mind that in rejecting a cushy provincial practice (that he had inherited by marriage in Rennes and which would have insured his financial security for a lifetime) in order to work among the dregs of society in the north side of Paris where he was paid irregularly for his private consultations and where he subsisted on a meager state salary earned by working in a public dispensary, he had come to know what poverty and deprivation were like. He would never get rich as a doctor. Like Bardamu, his hero in *Voyage,* education had changed the way he looked at the world and had given him a claim to the human respect of other people.

But deep down, like Robinson, Bardamu's alter ego, Céline refused to change and to go along with society. In a word, he was convinced — and this is perhaps his greatest moral claim to our human respect for him as a man — that to take advantage of the physical infirmity of his fellow human beings was to pervert the education that he had worked so hard to acquire. He thus cared for the ills of the human body for the rest of his life and did not even earn his subsistance from doing so. During those long years that

went into the creation of *Voyage,* years spent in devoting evenings
to the creation of the story of Bardamu/Robinson's dark journey,
after having spent his days caring for his fellow man's maladies,
Céline must surely have hoped that his book would make him some
money, that it would be read and talked about, and that in some
way he would be recompensed for his labor. For in turning his back
on the chance for an easy medical practice that would have insured
a healthy financial return in order to work for very little financial
compensation, he had decided to show by his actions what his novel
would say with words. It has become all too fashionable to say that
Céline was a terrible person but a gifted writer. While it is true that
he hardly had a sociable personality and refused to offer any higher
reasons or sentimental explanations for his work as a doctor, his
actions by themselves testify that despite all the shortcomings he
found in mankind, he was still committed to helping people —
without getting rich in the process. This must be said in his behalf.

Thus there is an element of truth in his assertion when he gives
the following reason for writing *Voyage*: "I'll never be able to say
it enough. My intention was to sell four or five thousand copies of a
real book and the income would have enabled me to be housed
decently."[7] There is some truth here, but it is not all truth either.
On the contrary, it is also a pose, a role Céline played during his
whole literary career. Not having been born a true proletarian, for
his family of *petit bourgeois* origin was neither really *bourgeois* nor
proletarian (a term which in France usually refers to salaried
manual workers who are very poorly paid in comparison with their
counterparts in this country), he opted at an early date for the role
of *petit prolo*. One of the things that first struck Dorian and Denoël
when they finally met Céline was his exaggerated Parisian accent,
an accent which to the refined French ear can be likened to the
effect that Cockney or Bronx intonations have on a British or
American ear. He used vulgar, slangy expressions in his daily
speech, adorned his literary production with the same kind of
language, and was as nondescript and as unimposing as possible in
his personal appearance, deliberately shunning fine clothes and
never owning an automobile (which he probably could have afforded quite easily). It is only logical then that he should maintain
the anti-intellectual facade completely by insisting that he had no
literary or intellectual intentions whatsoever in writing *Voyage*.
Céline from the very beginning had something of the Philistine

about him. No matter how obvious it would become over the years that he was telling a tall tale and insulting his reader or listener by evading the truth (i.e., that he must have had *some* literary ambition to write a book like *Voyage*), he still clung to his line. One wonders, the more one gets to know the man, how well truth and reality were separated in his own mind.

We cannot even begin to talk about *Voyage,* which is the story of a psychological and moral journey, without remembering to distinguish between the author, Doctor Destouches now become the novelist Céline, and his hero(es) Bardamu/Robinson. All of Céline's novels are deeply autobiographical, but the autobiographical element in them has been "transposed"[8] in the process of finding its way into literature. As we recount below the series of adventures that befall Bardamu as he gropes his way toward the end of his own night (night being death for Robinson and accommodation to society and deeper self-knowledge for Bardamu), the reader will see many parallels between these adventures and the ones which we know to have taken place in Céline's own life. The experience of reality, the memory and recall of actions, moods, and feelings, give birth in Céline to Bardamu's own experiences, but despite this fact we must do our utmost to keep the two lives as seperate as possible.

II *From An Insane World to a Mental Asylum*

Voyage opens with young Bardamu talking with his friend Arthur Ganate, a student like himself. It is a warm day and Ferdinand and Arthur notice that the streets around the usually busy café at the place Clichy where they are seated are deserted. That morning President Poincaré has been inaugurated, and from a piece of information like this we are able to situate the time of the action described by Céline, for he is miserly with dates and generally shuns any attempt at recreating a traditional and logical chronicling of the passage of time in his novels, preferring to picture time as one long deep haze through which his characters march. There are no calendars, clocks, or time whistles in his work. Time is forever present, constantly pressing down on his characters as they flee from its effect (it brings them inexorably closer to death), yet Céline consciously avoids talking about time in the traditional realistic mode.

Their conversation is interrupted by the passing of a military parade. Soldiers are marching through the streets of Paris, a colonel on horseback in the lead. Ferdinand Bardamu, enchanted by the appearance of the men and obviously deluded by what military life potentially holds in store for him, runs off and joins their company.

The brief opening four page section is over almost as fast as it had begun and in the next section of the book (in this, his first novel, Céline does not divide his book into chapters as such, but the text is nonetheless cut up into what we can call sections or episodes) we find Bardamu plunged *in media res*. He is in the army, the lines are drawn between the French and Germans, and like a rat in his hole he is being shot at by German snipers. As much as he strains his memory to try to recall what he personally might have against the Germans whom he is being asked to kill, he cannot remember one incident that could justify his presence in this absurd situation. "The war," he surmises, "in fact, was everything that one didn't understand. It couldn't go on." [9] But the war can and will go on, drawing Bardamu even more deeply into it. With bullets flying all about him in the bright autumn sunshine, and commanded by a general and a colonel who are loving every minute of the carnage, Ferdinand has a sudden realization of what death, which each bullet whistling past him can potentially bring, means to him: "If you've no imagination dying doesn't matter much; if you have, it's too much. That's what I think. Never had I understood so many things at once." [10] Dismayed when he sees his colonel killed, he calls out to an NCO that the colonel is dead. The petty officer, unconcerned, screams back that there are plenty of colonels around to replace that dead one and that Bardamu should get to work on the carcasses of a slain ox and of several pigs and sheep, chunks of which he has been designated to carry back to hungry men at the front. But the sight of raw meat, of sheep, pigs, and an ox being hacked to pieces, their stench engulfing the men who will shortly vie with millions of flies, thick and aggressive like sparrows, for the choicest morsels, is enough to make Bardamu faint. When he regains consciousness the bad dream has not ended. The war is still going on.

These opening pages devoted to the horror of war, of all war, not only of the modern mechanized kind, is heightened and intensified in the next section of the novel. The French armies are in flight. As will be the case in the rest of the novel, Céline makes no attempt to link Bardamu's experience with that of the larger entity of which he is but a small part. He is not interested in giving his reader an overview like, say, Jules Romains in *Verdun*,[11] for his way of making the general statement is not through description but by rendering the fear, horror, and revulsion of his hero so urgently concrete for the reader that through him one comes to share these feelings. We are in Flanders. Word has been given to fall back on a village named Barbigny. The war has been raging already for four weeks. At first Bardamu learns during these nocturnal retreats that generals sleep indoors while common soldiers are lodged in the open air, but after another month of this insane business there are no more villages or farmhouses left. Everything has been destroyed so that now everyone can sleep outside — even generals.

Although Bardamu now realizes that he had become sensible enough to see that cowardice— in other words, flight — was his only salvation, he will nonetheless be entrusted with a mission by his captain who sends him off alone in search of four other soldiers. Still a mile away from his destination, the village of Noirceur-sur-la-Lys,[12] he comes upon a farmhouse where a family sits in fear, waiting for death. The Germans have already passed through, killing one of their children on their way, and after Bardamu chats with them for a moment he goes in search of Noirceur. But before getting there he meets a strange man in the dark. Léon Robinson, a reservist called to active duty in the infantry, is, like Bardamu (a regular soldier in the cavalry), fed up with war and longing to be captured by the Germans. Together they head into the village in the hope that there the Germans will capture them, but the enemy, they soon learn, has not yet arrived. Disappointed, they part ways, each returning to his own war. But they will meet again many times before Bardamu's journey is over.

Just as Céline had used a jerky cinematographic technique earlier in the novel by cutting the scene of his hero on the café terrace on the place Clichy in order to transport him to an army camp, he continues to do the same thing here. Now, all of a sudden, Bardamu is in Paris among civilians. Ostensibly on leave of some kind, and enjoying the respite of life behind the lines, he encounters the first of several females who will mingle their lives with his in the course of the novel. This first one is named Lola, "la petite Lola d'Amerique," as he calls her, and she is a nurse with the American

Red Cross in Paris. They quickly become intimate and together discuss the war and its meaning. For her, a victim of wartime Allied propaganda, it is a crusade against barbarism, while for Bardamu it is all a big lie.

Wartime Paris, with its streets full of cripples and with propaganda posters everywhere, is almost as bad for him as the front lines. Lying, copulating, and dying is all life means to him, and with the dread of returning to the front slowly wearing down his resistance, Bardamu has a kind of nervous breakdown, after which he is handcuffed and dragged off to a hospital for observation. His illness, the doctors tell him, is that he has been "driven insane ... by fear. They may have been right. When one's in this world, surely the best thing one can do, isn't it, is to get out of it? Whether one's mad or not, frightened or not."[13] Of course, in such an insane situation as this, with people killing each other for reasons they do not understand, madness is simply having the bad luck to be in disagreement with the majority. When Lola comes to the hospital and tells Bardamu that he is nothing more than a coward or a madman for refusing to go to war when his homeland is in danger, he retorts, "Then long live all cowards and madmen!"[14] At this point the basic points of tension around which the whole novel will be structured have been established. The influence of the war experience convinces Bardamu of the madness of society. Thus, here and for the rest of the novel, his response will be flight each time he is overwhelmed by the madness of society.

After a while Bardamu will be allowed to wander from the hospital during the day. Lola is no longer on the scene and is soon replaced in Bardamu's life by Musyne, a prostitute, who works in the passage des Bérésinas, the fictional alley in which Ferdinand, the hero of Céline's second novel, *Death on the Installment Plan*, will grow up. Although she has virtually no feeling at all for him, Musyne agrees to take an apartment with Bardamu in the suburban area of Billancourt, but nonetheless continues to practice her trade elsewhere, until she finally turns her back completely on him, forsaking him for some wealthy Argentines.

All through these pages, as Bardamu learns about the deceptions he finds inherent in relations between men and women, Céline also uses his characters and situations to protest against misguided and exaggerated notions of patriotism. War, for him, is an inexcusable slaughter, and the people who speak most lyrically about it are either those who are safely ensconced behind the lines, or who, even better, are making money from it. War, Céline seems to be saying, is just another tool used by the classes that own wealth to maintain what they have and to keep the working classes poor, weak, and divided. There are two human groups on the earth, the rich and the poor, and in the case of Bardamu it had taken twenty years of life and the experience of the war to make this discovery. When you are poor, you learn to stick to your own group and to ask the price of everything, of people as well as of things, before getting involved with them. Perhaps it is for this reason that he now gets in touch with his mother, spending his free Sundays walking about the outskirts of Paris with her and wondering at her resigned optimism in the face of calamity. Symptomatic of the older generation that came to maturity prior to the war, she somehow feels that the horrible events that have visited so much suffering upon the common people have somehow been merited by them. Bardamu, in his newly gained lucidity, rejects such a view, and for this reason life will only become more burdensome for him.

After acquiring and then losing a third mistress, this one an actress who soon runs off with one of Bardamu's fellow inmates, Céline's hero takes a part time job working for a jeweler, Monsieur Puta, for whom he had worked before the war. There he meets an old friend Voireuse (also a soldier now, but on leave), who goes as often as he can to see an old couple who have lost a son at the front. Each time he sees them, Voireuse tells them of the fashion in which their son died, and the wife gives him 100 francs. But now, when he goes out to see the lady in Bardamu's company, they discover not only that the woman has died of sorrow (she was the one who gave the money, not her husband) but also that the father is talking to a soldier whom Bardamu instantly recognizes. It is Robinson, the fellow he had met earlier in Noirceur-sur-la-Lys and with whom he had tried to get captured. Now, also trying to get money out of this old couple, he exchanges greetings with Bardamu and then they wander off again in different directions. They of course will meet again, but Voireuse will be gassed a short time later.

III *Flight to Africa and the United States*

Given the structuring criterion we mentioned above — that is, the awareness of the world's insanity which prompts the hero to attempt to flee, and in the process has him end up in an asylum for those who, in the eyes of society, are disturbed — we can say that the first of the two main parts of the novel ends when, all of a sudden, and without giving us any reason for his release from the mental hospital, Bardamu first wanders around Paris a bit more and then makes his way to Africa. This will be the first of many fresh beginnings for Bardamu during the rest of the novel.

He has mixed feelings about starting out in the world by going off to tropical Africa, but anything is better than the insane international slaughterhouse from which he is escaping. The voyage is a strange one indeed, for his fellow passengers on the ship decide, for a reason that is never made clear to the reader, that Bardamu deserves their hatred. He is persecuted during the length of the trip by people who hardly know him but who decide that he will represent for them an outsider, a kind of scapegoat for their own frustrations. And right up until his arrival at the port of Fort-Gono, an oceanside settlement in the colony of Bambola-Bragamance (based on the Cameroons, where Céline lived for a while during the war), he will live in fear of losing his life at the hands of the soldiers aboard the *Amiral Bragueton* who have been turned against him by the women aboard ship. Once he is on land he learns that he will have to travel to a distant point, Topo, to assume his responsibilities with the Pardurière Lumber Company. But even before setting out, Bardamu learns of the effect the climate has on people who must live under its weight. His special concern, though, since he has little sympathy for the indigenous population, is with the effect of this tropical heat and humidity on the white businessmen and soldiers who must live there.

Once he gets to Topo, a ten day boat trip along the coast, he is able to see up close the difference between the two main conduits of French civilization in the colony, the soldier and the businessman. Céline reveals these two aspects of French colonial society through the persons of Lieutenant Grappa, the commander of the outpost who knows nothing of the interior (of which he is nonetheless the military commander), and Alcide, who engages in commerce with the indigenous population, saving the small profits he makes in order to send them back to France. In fact, with reference to Alcide, we find Bardamu expressing for the first time in the novel some human emotion, indeed genuine tenderness, with regard to the charitable acts of another human being. This reaction is provoked when he learns that Alcide is putting aside all his money, and is volunteering to remain six consecutive years in the colony (double the usual three) to better support a niece in Bordeaux who suffers from infantile paralysis.

But now Bardamu will have to leave the relatively easy life of Topo to travel inland to replace a company official who lives in the middle of the jungle. After a difficult journey, he will not immediately recognize the man he is replacing, but when the man tells him his name is Robinson, he begins to suspect that it is the same man he has already met twice before. Night falls with a thud over the jungle and, as Bardamu struggles to get to sleep, he realizes that this man is the same one whom he had accompanied to the edge of night in Flanders and whom he had later met in Paris. When daylight comes and Bardamu seeks to confront Robinson with his past, to ask him if he is indeed the man he has already met twice, he finds that Robinson has fled again.

Céline here stops his narrative for a moment to allow his hero to dwell on the meaning of this alter ego in his life. "Everything came back to me. Years sped by in a single moment. I had been very ill in the head, I'd been unhappy. ... Now that I knew, now that I had recognized him, I couldn't help being thoroughly alarmed. Had he known me? In any case, he could count on my silence, my complicity."[15] Bardamu is now aware for the first time that Robinson might not be as aware of him as he is of Robinson. In other words, as a fictional device, Céline is telling his reader that Robinson is the outgrowth of Bardamu's inner psychological processes and that the reverse is not the case. This explains why Robinson was in the army at the same time as Bardamu and then later on had leave time in Paris at the same time as Bardamu. Now, like Bardamu, he has been living in Africa for a year and hates virtually everything about the place. But why does Robinson appear clearly to Bardamu's awareness only on certain selected occasions? And do these instances of apparition have anything in common?

The answers to these two questions are not too difficult to arrive at, for Céline has made it quite clear from the first appearance of Robinson in the narrative that Robinson presents himself to Bardamu's consciousness only in moments of stress or of self-doubt. First, when Bardamu is literally alone in no man's land between French and German lines, his alter ego appears to him and together they try to get themselves captured — a wish that Bardamu had secretly harbored from the moment he first understood the absurdity of the mad international slaughterhouse that was war. Robinson, unlike Bardamu, goes ahead and does things that someone used to the ways of society (even if, like Bardamu he realizes their arbitrariness and even downright foolishness) does not readily dare to do. Bardamu had already given much thought to deserting but did not actually dare to try to go over to the Germans and try to get himself captured until he saw that Robinson had no compunction about such an act. Likewise, when Bardamu is later led along by Voireuse to take advantage of someone else's intense suffering to extort a few francs for himself — in other words, when he is led to commit such an act by his friend — he finds that someone else has already beat them to the punch. Robinson has already arrived on the scene and is trying shamelessly to make one hundred francs for himself in exactly the same way that Bardamu — at the urging of Voireuse — has decided that he will try to pad his own wallet.

Now, finally, at the edge of despair in the middle of the jungle, Bardamu remembers that the occasions on which he had met Robinson were moments in which he had been "very ill in the head," and "unhappy." Robinson, from a psychological point of view is a symbol of self-awareness and lucidity. He represents Bardamu's ability to see into himself and to find the difference between his conscious self, accustomed now for over thirty years to living up to (no matter how imperfectly and begrudgingly) the dictates of society, and that other self, a kind of id, that has undergone no process of socialization. Significantly, Robinson is so outrageous in his conduct that he does not hesitate to massage the thighs of the little black boys who are forever waiting on him. Bardamu's sexual activities, on the other hand, are always heterosexual in nature. But Robinson could not care less: he shows no concern whatsoever for what society asks from people. He does what he wants.[16]

Spurred on by Robinson's disappearance, Bardamu once again decides to flee. Sick and delirious with fever, he has himself carried for several days on a stretcher to the border of Bragamance and Rio del Rio, the neighboring colony. There he comes under the care and influence of a Spanish priest in the city of San Tapeta and in due course the clergyman sells him into slavery. Bardamu is bought by the captain of a slave galley, the *Infanta Combitta*, and spends weeks rowing his way he knows not where. He wonders vaguely if Robinson is aboard and, although he cannot find him when he searches about the ship for him, he feels strangely confident that Robinson has been shipped off to the same destination on a separate galley. He calls out Robinson's name several times in the middle of the night but there is no answer. The rowing continues, the journey seems truly now to be without end, and then one day, telling us that "I was no longer delirious,"[17] Bardamu looks up to find that the *Infanta Combitta* has finally reached port. He gapes out the porthole of his slave galley and what does he find but the vertical monsters of the New York skyline!

This whole passage, and it takes up only about three pages, is the first use in Céline's fiction of a "delirium" scene. Earlier in the novel Bardamu had undergone a kind of psychological crisis that led up to his being put in a mental hospital but that scene was not developed the same way this one is. Here, Céline clearly tells us that his hero is in a state of delirium. He has taken leave of his senses. Any semblance of reasonable control of his mind or of his actions has been suspended. His imagination is set free to roam as it wishes and the explosion of words that describes the clearly unreasonable occurrences that he describes on board ship introduces us here to a fresh Célinian technique, one that he would exploit with growing ability in his future work. But here the delirium scene is used mainly to get his hero from Africa to New York in as direct a way as possible — by way of delirium, Céline's route of the unhinged mind, of the liberated and lyrical imagination. Thus, delirium in *Voyage* is an essential part of the structure of the novel, for it is linked both to madness and to evasion.

After a brief period of time in quarantine, Bardamu elects to go through Ellis Island and settle for a time in the United States. The other galley slaves reproach him for having anything to do with this strange land in the New World — which evokes once again the fresh beginning that Baramu seems always willing to attempt. His adventures in New York are basically of the nomadic variety for he will not stay there very long. Living in a cheap hotel in the Times Square area, he goes from there on walks about the city, exploring rundown movie houses and sleazy hot dog joints, and discovering other unusual places for a visitor, like the public rest room in the subway stop at City Hall station. The page devoted to the natural functions being exercised in this place is outrageously funny, but the humor can not deceive the reader, for all the while Bardamu is withdrawing deeper and deeper into himself. He is overwhelmed by the beauty of the women he encounters in the streets of New York, but his own inability to reach out and touch what he admires only turns him back in upon himself. Alone, he conjures up in his imagination a blonde beauty he had seen in the movies and masturbates. But when this brings him neither comfort nor distraction, he realizes that he is sounding the very depths of despair. He is getting older and, maddeningly alone, he is going nowhere. For the time being, his journey has no goal other than death, but he does hint that self-understanding might be a legitimate goal. However, this also he now equates with self-delusion: "Truth is a pain that will not stop. And the truth of this world is to die. You must choose, either dying or lying. Personally, I have never been able to kill myself."[18] The only thing that allows a person to distract himself from this grim fact of death is "délire," or delirium, but, as Bardamu realizes, he seems to be running short for the moment of a sufficient amount of delirium to go against the tide of society.[19] "Délire" in this sense seems to be one's own provision of self-respect — or self-delusion, if you will — that enables the individual to face up to a hostile exterior reality. Thus far it has become clear that Bardamu has considered suicide but has been unable to bring himself to do it. He thus remains open to accommodation with society, and for another attempt at a fresh start. Before long he rediscovers Lola who is now a prostitute living on Seventy-seventh Street in Manhattan. But she, like the officers on the *Amiral Bragueton*, will show him nothing but contempt. Still, he manages to extract a hundred dollars from her to embark on a new beginning, this time on a Ford assembly line in Detroit.

Céline's strongest statements about capitalism and the effect that this economic system has on the poor and exploited are reserved for these final pages of Bardamu's adventures in America. Working for a salary of six dollars a day, he finds himself so dehumanized by work on the assembly line that he can do no more than go to the movies like a zombie during his free evenings. But then he meets Molly, a prostitute endowed with such prodigious energy that she herself earns a hundred dollars a day for her labor. Her devotion to Ferdinand over the next few weeks is such that he feels guilty when he senses welling up inside himself the desire to return home in order to continue his education. "I was even rather ashamed of all the trouble she took to hold me. I was very fond of her, of course, that's certainly true, but I was fonder still of my own obsession, of my longing to run away from everywhere in search of something, God knows what; prompted no doubt by stupid pride, by a conviction of some kind of superiority."[20]

In this situation, feeling tense about what he will do next, Bardamu senses that a meeting with Robinson is imminent. When he stops by the French Consulate to ask if Robinson is in the country, he is told that the authorities are in fact on the lookout for him because of his false identity papers. Then, not surprisingly, the two meet again, but this time it is Robinson who calls out first to Bardamu. Troubled, but clearly less desperate than he had been on each of the previous occasions he had met Robinson — and on which he had seen Robinson first, before being seen by the latter — he now learns that it is Robinson who is in trouble. Unhappily employed as a janitor working nights in office buildings, Robinson sees no way out of his predicament. With his false identification papers it is he — that part of Bardamu that usually appears only at moments of extreme distress — who is hopeless with regard to the future. While the partially socialized Bardamu is looking forward to returning home to attempt once again a compromise with society, that other side of himself is doing everything to keep from going back. But now that Bardamu is in complete control of himself, Robinson vanishes from the narrative. Finally, when Ferdinand takes leave of Molly, we have what is probably the most tender scene in all of Céline's work. Molly understands and accepts that for Bardamu at this point in his life the most important thing is for him to do exactly what he feels he has to do. He leaves, feeling sad for himself, for her, and for all men, and then the narrative leaps forward in time.

Many years have passed, and the narrator tells us that for years now he has tried to regain contact with Molly but to no avail. "Good, admirable Molly, I should like her, if she ever reads these lines of mine, to know for certain that I have not changed towards her, that I love her still and always shall, in my own way. ..."[21] Here, for the first time in Céline's fiction, his hero actually feels "love" for another human being. The point is worth mentioning in passing, for Céline is all too often dismissed as a writer totally consumed by hatred. We might also point out here that this flight from Molly's arms illuminates clearly that the "night" of the title of this novel represents not only death, death of the body and thus of the mind when one's biological system breaks down, but also self-understanding, self-acceptance, and accommodation with society. When Bardamu leaves Molly behind, it is to do what every man must ultimately do: "become oneself truly before death." [22] In the moving farewell to Molly, the "je" of the now hardened narrator seems to be speaking more with the voice of Céline than of Bardamu when he says: "I was sad for once, really sad, sad for everybody, for myself, for her, for all men." [23]

IV *The Return to France and to an Asylum*

A foul odor and a sour taste, these are the images conjured up by the French adjective "ranci." As the next section of the novel opens, Bardamu has already completed his medical studies and is trying to squeeze a living out of a private practice in the suburbs to the north of Paris, the area that has come to be called the "Red Belt" because of the strength the French Communist Party has continued to have among the dispossessed who live just outside the city. During the thirties these suburbs continued to swallow up all available land, with shanties springing up rapidly across a landscape which, before World War I, had been a relatively wide open space. The people who came to live in these areas were for the most part people who could not afford to live elsewhere, and it is among these folk, the lowest on the socioeconomic scale, that Bardamu, like Céline incidentally, chose to work. But if life in Rancy, has "turned," just as butter, say, has "turned," rancid, it is because the people living there are for the most part poor. In fact, it is unfair to Céline to say, as some critics have, that he is a nihilist who hates all manifestations of the human kind. That is not quite true, for, in this novel at least, occasional flashes of sunlight and of fresh air break through to enliven the atmosphere somewhat, an atmosphere that is mainly conditioned by poor education and low socioeconomic profiles.

Céline said on several occasions that Eugène Dabit's success with *Hôtel du Nord* (1929) inspired him to try his hand at novel writing. Although no one ever seems to have taken this assertion too seriously, there is still quite a bit of truth in it as far as this next section of *Voyage* is concerned. In these pages, Céline uses a technique quite close to the one employed by Dabit in his first novel. For just as the latter used the hotel located in a working class district of Paris on the quai Saint-Martin as the locus around which he told in brief, hard-hitting, but otherwise unrelated chapters, of the moral and physical poverty of the inhabitants of the hotel, so also Céline uses the character of Bardamu as a doctor treating the same kinds of people in order to introduce us into the domestic life of a series of dreary lower class characters. Significantly, Robinson is absent (he will only reappear when Bardamu discovers that his attempts to interact decisively with society are a dismal failure) throughout this whole section of the novel, a section which through the aptness and forcefulness of its naturalistic detail plunges the reader up to his neck in the reality of what life is like for a doctor who refuses to get rich on the misfortune of others and thus willingly chooses as his clientele that section of the population that is not only least able to pay — but also, he discovers, often least willing to do so.

Despite the presence of too many other doctors in the neighborhood, or so he is told, Bardamu still sets up shop in this unhappy district. Among the characters he encounters are Bébert, the concierge in a nearby apartment building who lives with his aunt, a hateful witch of a person addicted to ether who is forever telling people that Bardamu is incompetent; and the Henrouilles, another family consisting of a man and his wife who have lived their whole life scrimping and saving for retirement and who, once they do retire, live in terror of dying. Callously, the latter lock up Mr. Henrouille's mother in a shed behind their tiny house for she is "crazy," which is another way of saying that they want to get rid of her because she is too much of a bother. But when the Henrouilles call on Bardamu to sign a paper testifying that she is mentally incompetent and should be sent to an institution, Bardamu cannot bring himself to do it. Another call is to care for a young woman who has just performed her third abortion on herself and is at death's door. When Dr. Bardamu saves her life, her parents are reluctant to pay him — an occurrence that happens quite frequently to Bardamu for by his own admission he has not learned how to demand his money. After this he is called upon in an emergency to minister to a child, a little girl who has been cruelly beaten by her sadistic parents. This ritual, we learn, is usually followed by a lovemaking scene between the parents as the child lies whimpering on the floor.

The power of these scenes is, frankly, overwhelming and they are responsible in large part for making *Voyage* one of the most forceful novels in French literature. Their effect on the reader is so potent that one wonders how Bardamu, knowing him by now as we do, can manage to bear up under such pressure, living in penury himself, despised by the people he is treating, and having to deal with the dregs of society, with people whose image of themselves is not far removed from excrement, whose odor literally surrounds their lives. No wonder then that Bardamu starts to tell us that "nobody will get it out of my head," for, "the idea of meeting Robinson again had come to me with a shock; it was like a sort of illness getting hold of me again." [24] Whenever Bardamu falters in his attempts to deal with society and to face up to the madness of the "sane" world, Robinson's appearance is not far off. Robinson, symbol of an unchanging, primitive, almost Darwinian attitude toward life according to which you get others before they get you, wells to the surface each time that Bardamu fails in his struggle to face up to what society expects of him.

These pages, like the ones devoted to Bardamu's adventures in Detroit, are replete with references to the poverty of the working classes with whom Bardamu deals every day. He has taken a job in a clinic where he specializes in treating tuberculosis cases. Bardamu has been a failure at private practice, just as he had failed as a soldier and as a commercial agent in Africa, but he has not given up completely yet. The ultimate dream of his patients is to be declared unable to work so they can then gain a government pension for the rest of their days. For this reason, he eventually gets over his bad habit of promising health to his patients, for then their poverty would still remain. But completely different from these people are the rich, who are well fed and generally better to look at. All men, rich and poor, must eventually face death, but the wealthy have a means other than the poor man's alcohol with which to forget about death for "to be rich is another form of intoxication: it spells forgetfulness." [25] The poor, however, are fed and nourished on illusion. They breed like animals, living and dying and being exploited generation after generation.

The one bright light in Bardamu's life at this time is the adolescent boy Bébert. "A smile of pure affection which I have never been able to forget danced on his glistening little face. A gay thing for the world to see." [26] To the poverty stricken doctor disillusioned by what he sees in adult conduct every day, there is less risk involved in attachment to a child than to an adult. But when Bardamu finds himself unable to treat the particular form of typhoid fever that the boy suffers from, he decides that he will consult a specialist.

He thus takes a day off and goes in to Paris to visit a friend of his, Parapine, who is doing medical research at the "Institut." But what a disappointment this trip is, for Parapine is even more skeptical than Bardamu at this point about the efficacy of any human endeavor. All he wants from life at this moment in his existence is to continue to draw his paycheck until it is all over. He no longer has any professional ambitions — nor does he believe any more in what he is doing. After this visit, Bardamu returns home depressed once again. Shortly thereafter, Robinson is back again. For days on end he comes to chat with Bardamu, who is in a terrible state of depression. Strangely, he is usually accompanied by old lady Henrouille, the eighty year old whose life Bardamu had refused to consign to an institution. Finally, Bardamu and Robinson spend a Sunday afternoon together on a café terrace listening to American music — the one thing that Robinson learned to appreciate during his two years in the United States. For him, just as for Bardamu (and for the American people as a whole we are told), music is the universal painkiller, the necessary invention to dispel the pain and monotony of existence.

But then Robinson disappears again and that night Bardamu is called out for two emergencies, one to treat a man dying of cancer and the other, in the same building, two flights up, for a woman bleeding to death of a miscarriage. After the first patient dies, Bardamu wants the second one to be transported to the hospital but her husband cannot make up his mind to have her treated elsewhere. Depressed, Bardamu gives up and leaves the house. Once again Robinson appears on the scene and in the following conversation he reveals to Bardamu that Mr. and Mrs. Henrouille have hired him to assassinate old lady Henrouille. The repressed side of Bardamu's character is now contracting to do what Bardamu, prompted by professional conscience, would never contemplate. When Bardamu asks Robinson how he ever got involved with the Henrouilles, he answers that he met the old lady first in Bardamu's waiting room. Robinson, that dark side of Bardamu's character, is now taking advantage of this poor old woman who had been saved by the socially adapted Bardamu. His plan is to set a bomb to the door of the hutch in the Henrouille's back yard. When the old lady goes out to feed the rabbits, the bomb will go off in her face and she will be disposed of.

In the course of this conversation, Robinson also reveals to Bardamu that he would have liked to become a nurse himself because as a medical practitioner it is easier to deal with people: "because, you know, when people are well, there's no getting away from it, they're rather frightening. ... Especially since the war ... I know what they're thinking. ... They don't always realize it themselves. But I know. When they can stand up, they're thinking of killing you. Whereas when they're ill, there's no doubt about it, they're less dangerous. You've got to be prepared for them to do any damned thing while they're well — isn't that so?" [27] And on reflection Bardamu discovers that "perhaps Robinson was right," [28] and that deep within himself the reason why he, Bardamu, chose to enter medicine was perhaps in part to better defend himself against others.

A short while later the attempted assassination of poor old lady Henrouille is aborted when Robinson's bomb explodes in his own face, blinding him. In search of a solution to their problem, the Henrouilles now successfully bribe Bardamu to convince Robinson to leave Paris and go south with the old woman to Toulouse, where together they will work as tourist guides in the basement of an old church. Bardamu, who for one hundred francs would not sign a paper putting old lady Henrouille in an institution, now insists on two thousand francs to get rid of Robinson for the Henrouilles. Robinson is out of the way and Bardamu has once again fought off his latest fit of depression — but he is also barely able to make a living and is also a criminal.

In taking the bribe from the Henrouilles, he, like Molly the prostitute for instance, is doing something that the law, although it often looks the other way in matters such as these, still does not sanction. Robinson had never been afraid of breaking the law and now Bardamu, for the first time, joins him in this respect. For the older narrator of the novel there are only two kinds of people who have received any sympathy so far. On the one hand there are the prostitute Molly and the colonial agent Alcide, both of whom technically break the law in their work, and then there are the innocent Bébert and the "mad" old lady Henrouille whose tenacity toward life is warmly portrayed. Bardamu has now gone over the boundary that separates him from those who, despite constant disillusionment and setback, still try to conform to the norms of conduct set by society. The immediate and dramatic recent failure in his life has been his inability to save Bébert. But now, not only does he seem ready to abandon his job as an agent of healing, he has also taken a bribe. Since by his act he has joined the company of Molly and Alcide, the question can also be asked as to whether he will now also go mad, and in so doing join the company of someone like old lady Henrouille, who is considered "mad" by others but who is nevertheless able to hold on to life despite the desire of her own son to do away with her.

Robinson is gone and Bardamu cannot earn a living in private practice. His physical health is now in jeopardy, too, for he feels weak and suffers from a cold he cannot get rid of. When Bébert's aunt finally pays him a sum of money she owes him, he spends ten days in bed resting and thinking and decides that the time has come to pack up and go elsewhere. He abandons his office and wanders toward the place Clichy, a large square in the north end of Paris where, we recall, the novel had begun, and near where its action will also end. Here he enters a vaudeville theater, the Tarapout, where he meets Parapine again, and before the evening is over he accepts a job as a walk on extra. Earning his living in a world of fantasy and make believe while residing in a hotel, he spends all his free time exploring the world of sensuality under the guidance of the great pimp Pomone. Here too, though, sadness eventually overwhelms him: "Life, just by itself — what a dirge that is! Life is a classroom and Boredom's the usher, there all the time to spy on you; whatever happens, you've got to look as if you were awfully busy all the time doing something that's terribly exciting — or he'll come along and nibble your brain. A day that is nothing but a mere round of twenty-four hours isn't to be borne. It has to be one long, almost unbearable thrill, a twenty-four hour copulation."[29]

Since Bardamu has now reached another impasse in which even a life of total emersion in physical pleasure leads nowhere (it is important to note that Robinson, for whom sex means almost nothing, is away all this time), he will liberate himself through the use of a second delirious dream. As he falls asleep he is with Tania, a Polish dancer from the Tarapout. They are in a café at the place du Tertre in Montmartre. The cemetery nearby reminds him of death and, in a delirious four page explosion of words and images, he sees pass before his eyes former patients from Paris and other assorted characters from his adventures in Africa and America. All dead, they now file through his imagination. Molly, however, his one hope in life, is absent from the delirious dream through which Bardamu succeeds in killing off his past in order to start afresh once more. Importantly, in both delirium sequences Robinson is absent and cannot be readily contacted by Bardamu. It is this inner frustration, this dislocation of the total self, that leads to the frenzied state of delirium. Also, just as the first delirium scene had transported him from the Old World to the New World, so this one will transport him from the sleazy life of Rancy and the Tarapout to Toulouse where he will taste for the first time a few of the delights of a comfortable *bourgeois* existence.

When Tania wakes Dr. Bardamu from his troubled slumber, he confesses that "the thought of Robinson came back to plague me."[30] He returns to the old neighborhood and meets the Henrouilles, but Mr. Henrouille is about to die. Once he is dead, Bardamu and Mrs. Henrouille, who had tried to get along with each other until that point, finally have a falling out over her dead husband's dental plate. Now, thanks to an advance from the local priest, Father Protiste, Bardamu will be able to leave for Toulouse to visit with Robinson. When he gets there he learns that he and old lady Henrouille are indeed working at the Church of Saint Epinome guiding tourists through the lower vault where they can look at the mummies preserved there. But since he left Paris, Robinson had become engaged to a local twenty year old who now works along with him and old lady Henrouille. When Bardamu arrives he succeeds in seducing the girl, Madelon, so named because she was born during the war and thus has no fear of death, having been exposed to it since birth.

Robinson is probably aware of what is going on but he really does not seem to care for he has steadfastly retained his ability to say no to human attachment. As the uncivilized and uncivilizable side of Bardamu's character, he is willing to get married only on his own terms. Love need not be involved. Still cynical, he has adapted to his environment: he seeks nothing more than money, comfort, and a life of ease independent of society. Baradamu is revolted by this revelation and states: "I no longer listened to him. To tell the truth, he disappointed and rather disgusted me. 'You're respectable middle class,' I came to the conclusion. ... 'You really have no thought for anything beyond money ... by the time you get your eyesight back you'll be nastier than the rest of them.'" [31] Robinson, following a kind of blind instinct that pushes him to preserve and defend himself first and to give no thought whatsoever to others, almost as if he were some kind of blind irrational organism visible only with the aid of a microscope, is once again ahead of Bardamu. The latter, still journeying in search of some meaning to his existence, has not yet been able to say no in the absolute way that Robinson has made that negative statement. Bardamu, although hardly reconciled to society, is still theoretically reconcilable. As for Robinson, no accommodation is possible. He remains a rebel concerned with preserving his independence from society at all costs.

Bardamu would love to stay in Toulouse. Life is easy there, but he must get on his way, for money is running out and he needs more of it to keep alive. He still cannot drop out completely. Before going though he has a unique and significant experience while walking down the street with Robinson. He notices that people show on their faces a concern for the blind man — a kind of concern that Bardamu had never given much thought to before. He muses: "There's pity in people for the blind and infirm; they really have got love in reserve. I'd often felt the presence of this love in reserve. There's any amount of it. No good saying there isn't. Only it's a pity people should still be such sods, with so much love in reserve. It stays where it is, that's what. It's stuck away inside and it doesn't come out, doesn't do them any good. They die of love — inside." [32] This passage, usually overlooked in Céline criticism, expresses the compassion that Céline, the older narrator of the novel, felt for humanity and proved by his incessant labors as a medical doctor catering to those generally too poor to pay.

No wonder then that Bardamu, before taking leave of Robinson, should try to peer deeply into himself (i.e., look deeply into Robinson, who is really nothing more than his own subconscious) and to describe what he sees there. Does he, like "people" in general, have any residue of goodness and pity there to be tapped for the benefit of others? Sitting down with Madelon before his departure, he sets out "to define Robinson's temperament, as if I myself really knew what he was like, but I realized immediately that I didn't know Robinson at all." [33] Implied at this point in the novel, with Bardamu willing to recognize some good in people and in life while Robinson refuses to compromise his dark vision, is the notion that somehow Bardamu will have to get rid of Robinson. The latter, if Bardamu is to come to some kind of truce with society, will have to be conquered or subjugated in some way.

Now, just as Bardamu is about to buy his train ticket back to Paris, Robinson and Madelon convince him to stay for another week to see the countryside around Toulouse. He agrees and, after an outing a few days later, the day ends with Robinson and Madelon discussing their future while Bardamu strangely looks on. Both Léon Robinson and Madelon agree that Bardamu's conduct is a bit strange at times, that he is not the kind of man to be faithful to one woman, and that his mind is generally riveted on sex. Robinson goes along with everything Madelon wants him to say, even assuring her that when his sight returns completely (by this time it is already improving), he will be faithful to her alone. Bardamu, of course, could never be counted on for faithfulness, she asserts. The scene, a bizarre one that continues this *dédoublement* of Bardamu's consciousness back upon itself, points out once again that Bardamu and Robinson have less and less in common as time goes by. Robinson, although physically blind, is more than ever lucidly in search of financial and social security and independence and will stop at nothing to attain them. Bardamu, however, is still ill at ease with himself. They return to Toulouse at the end of the day's outing [34] and two days later Madame Henrouille mysteriously falls down the stairs to the church crypt and dies. Bardamu then leaves town without saying goodbye to anyone.

Perhaps Bardamu had been tending from the very beginning of his adventure to eventually end up in an insane asylum. Out of step with society and so ill at ease with himself that he had always felt torn and divided in two, it was only logical that his very sanity should eventually be called into question. He returns to Paris and has no stomach for going back to Rancy to practice among those he would rather not have to face any more. The Tarapout? No, there is no use going there either, for the economic crisis has already hit (by now it seems to be early in 1929) and jobs are not as readily available as they had been earlier. So Parapine, who now works for a Dr. Baryton, the owner of an asylum for disturbed people, comes to the rescue when he agrees to hire Bardamu. The latter's function, aside from having the right to copulate with the nurses as often as he wants, will be to administer electric shock treatments to the patients and to use the cinema — an invention of Parapine's — in treating their mental problems.

Dr. Baryton takes a liking to Bardamu and asks him to give his daughter English lessons. Although the girl is hardly interested in learning the language, her father begins to read, under Bardamu's direction, about the literature and history of England. After eight months he is so inflamed by this new interest that he is ready to give up his asylum and turn it over to Bardamu while he goes off to England to continue his work. After all, he says, "Have you not always been on the best of terms with our clients?" [35] So Bardamu is left in the suburb of Vigny-sur-Seine as director of the asylum, living among people who, in the eyes of society, are mad. The second part of the novel is now coming to a conclusion. Where Bardamu ended up being a patient in an asylum in the first part of the work, in the second part he is the director of an institution.

From Father Protiste, Bardamu gets word that Madame Henrouille has probably been murdered — having been pushed down the stairs to her death by Robinson instead of falling. But Bardamu is not surprised, for he had suspected as much all along. But what he did not suspect was that Robinson would soon be coming back to haunt him. Sure enough, soon after Baryton's departure, and just as Bardamu is settling into a predictable routine in his new position, Robinson returns to tell him that he has fled from Madelon and her mother. Now that he can see again, he has no intention of getting married. Many months pass during which Bardamu and Robinson work together with their patients, but despite the superficial calm, the inevitable restlessness remains within, for "morally speaking, our consciences weren't easy either. There were too many ghosts, one way or another." [36]

Then Madelon comes looking for her fiancé. Robinson remains in hiding, but when Bardamu finally gets to talk to her he expresses himself in a way that he had always wanted to conduct himself with another human being. He takes out all of his repressed aggression on her and lands "two slaps on her that would have been enough to shake a house." [37] For twenty years or more he had always wanted to react to somebody that way but had always held back. Undaunted, Madelon keeps on coming back until the moment she gets a chance to take her revenge on Robinson by shooting him. Although Bardamu by this time has found sexual gratification with

Sophie, a new employee of the asylum, he is more than ever aware of his loneliness as, near the avenue de Clichy, he watches Robinson die before his eyes. "But there was nobody but me, really me, just me, by his side, — a quite real Ferdinand who lacked what might make a man greater than his own trivial life, a love for the life of others. I hadn't any of that, or truly so little of it that it wasn't worth showing what I had. I wasn't death's equal. I was far too small for it. I had no great conception of humanity."[38]

At this point, with Robinson dead, the novel is about to end. Bardamu has no more to say and has even come to distrust words — they only get you into trouble anyway. Unlike Robinson, he has no great idea to live, and therefore to die, by. It was thanks to Robinson's great idea, he tells us, that he ended up getting himself killed, but Bardamu does not tell us what that great idea — that "really superb idea that was definitely stronger than death"[39] — consisted of. We can guess however, that it was Robinson's single-minded resolve to say no to life, to society, to human involvement, and to do anything to maintain his independence from others. It got him killed in the end; but to Bardamu's mind being dead means that the journey is over and thus that, in one sense, one has gone farther in life than someone like Bardamu who is still alive.

V   *Meaning and Structure of* Voyage

When the narrative ends, Bardamu's wanderings break off with the words, "let's not talk about it anymore,"[40] and we have in this declaration a prefigurement of one of the main streams of twentieth century literature. Life is too absurd, according to this view, to even talk about it any more. No novel until the appearance of *Voyage* had expressed so powerfully the sense of aimlessness and senselessness that characterizes so much of modern literature and modern life. Since then, sometimes perhaps without realizing it, many writers have continued to work the vein first struck so successfully by Céline, but he has not gotten full credit for the pioneering nature of his work. As Walter Orlando has written, "an original work of art whose influence is felt too immediately ends up becoming lost among its own offspring."[41]

To J. H. Matthews, "Bardamu's experience represents that of twentieth century man, conscious of his condition, yet unable to reconcile himself to it. ... In a world he can make no sense of,

Bardamu is groping for something which will give meaning to life.''[42] The underlying philosophy of the work is thus one of atheistic despair, for in a world where one sees no ultimate value either in man's ability to make sense out of life from within the framework of his existence or through the belief in a God who, from the outside, could confer some meaning on it all, the hero (or, as we say nowadays, antihero), would seem to have nothing to look forward to but death. But for Céline and Bardamu there is something else to be gained from life: self-understanding. And while it is not an absolute value, it is nonetheless a value. In this sense, the death of Robinson, Bardamu's alter ego, is an absolute necessity if Bardamu is to go on living. To Céline, Robinson represents that part of Bardamu's character that a man of science like himself could compare to the unthinking, instinctive cells he had often observed under a microscope. On a human plane this blind, primitive, and uncivilized force always sought satiation of its own drives before all else.

Where Bardamu usually hesitates to act, Robinson goes right ahead and does what he wants, and where Bardamu likes to think himself superior to Robinson (for instance, when he tells Léon that he is becoming a comfortable *bourgeois* during his stay in Toulouse), Robinson pays him no heed and holds on to Madelon as long as it is in his interest to do so. While blind and in need of her help he stays with her, but once he gets his sight back, he leaves her and refuses to marry her. Bardamu, right up to the very end, to the moment when the pain becomes so intense that he cannot even bear to speak any more, nonetheless continues to operate within society as best he can. He runs an asylum and makes his living from work, just as, earlier, he had gone out and acquired his medical degree and attempted to earn his living by having a private practice for a while. Robinson, however, has never wasted his time in such pursuits. Before he went to Africa and then on to America he had been a prisoner — or so he tells Bardamu at one point. Then, deserting the army, he had no compunction about travelling to America with false identity papers. Twice he tried to kill old lady Henrouille when money was at stake and the second time he succeeded. Ferdinand would never dream of actually doing any of these things, and in fact the most violent thing he does in the novel is to strike Madelon once, but even after that he eventually feels remorse. Robinson, on the other hand, conducts himself in such a way that he can never be too afraid that death is far off. As a criminal and later a murderer, as a man who at all times seeks to maintain total independence from society, or from "others" as Sartre would later put it, he is inevitably courting a final reckoning, for society does not tolerate such radical loners for very long. In this sense, we can say that Robinson, unlike Bardamu who continues to lie in order to continue to accept life (and this is probably the essence of the predicament of the modern antihero), cannot be called a liar. In fact, if anything, he possesses a lucid ability to stick to his own selfish course of action that Bardamu does not have. To Kingsley Widmer, Robinson's strong, steadfast refusal to go along can be called his "rigor of refusal." [43]

Céline, writing from a strong antisocial position in the novel, sees the world as divided between rich and poor, with all the good cards being stacked in favor of the former. Bardamu/Robinson belong to this world of the underdog and, as Widmer sees it, "their only real hope for human dignity is to overcome that feeling of obedience which the established in society demand. If the exploited have truly denied complicity in and acceptance of the vicious and fraudulent social authority, then they can boast of not having lived in vain. The basic idea: the nobility of refusal." [44] Of course, all through our commentary on this novel we have stressed the metaphysical side of this refusal to comply, and indeed the two strands, the social revolt and the metaphysical rejection of complicity, are woven deeply together, for the rich, as Bardamu well understands, benefit from an ability to forget the absurdity of life by the very fact that they have money. While to be poor is to be lost to vice and drowned in alcohol, to be rich is another form of intoxication: forgetfulness.

In succeeding pages we shall analyze and comment upon other of Céline's novels, but perhaps we should be forthright from the outset and state directly that for us *Voyage* is his masterpiece. This is so because all of Céline's great themes are present and are suspended, as in a chemical solution, in a happy balance. His ideas on delirium, first sketched out vaguely in *Semmelweis* and *L'Eglise*, reach a maturity of artistic expression here that will not be surpassed in his later work. His social revolt is total and irrevocable against a class system that not only divides the rich from the poor, but also finds it necessary through alcohol, the cinema, sporting events, and other highly advertised public diversions, including sex, to rock the exploited off to sleep in a kind of materialistic dreamworld where they will no longer think about their real interests.

Voyage is also the novel of a young man in search of his place in the world. With *Mort à crédit*, it is part of a *Bildungsroman* and, in this reader's view, it is not nearly so pessimistic a work as some would have us believe. After all, Bardamu does learn the value of work. He is never without a job for long and his constant search for employment and the emphasis that he puts on it indicate his understanding of the potential salutary effects that work can have for him — just as it can for any mature adult. Given his poor educational background and his low socioeconomic origins, his struggle to find an identity for himself is as modern and meaningful for the reader of today as it was over forty years ago. The use of Robinson as a foil, a reminder that there are two ways to face up to society — in a civilized way, which, after all, is Bardamu's way, or Robinson's way, the way of blind self-interest — is a successful device. Robinson's way cannot lead very far, and for this reason he must die before the end of the novel. In contrast, Bardamu, for all his failures and failings, is still alive and struggling when the book comes to an end, even though he has once again reached an impasse. It is important to recall, though, as we read to the end of *Voyage*, that Bardamu has not completely given up, for if he had, he would commit suicide. He might be lying to himself in order to find the strength to go on living, but in this respect he is the quintessential modern man living in our twentieth century, post-Christian society. Everybody, like Bardamu, must lie a little just to survive, or, as Céline put it so succinctly: "You must choose: either dying or lying. Personally, I have never been able to kill myself" (*Journey,* p. 199).

There are other dimensions to *Voyage*, though, that will forever make it a monument of modern fiction. The theme of pacifism, of a total rejection of war as a means of solving problems, is unconditional. As we read the opening pages of the novel, with its vivid and ironic descriptions of the butchery of modern warfare, we cannot help but be moved. People who do not know each other and who have no reason whatsoever for wanting to destroy each other find themselves ordered onto a battlefield in the name of values — flag, homeland, honor — that mean nothing to them and which, since the writing of *Voyage*, have come to mean even less to succeeding generations. Bardamu's discovery of the insanity of war among supposedly civilized nations is shared with us, and we, like him, reject this civilization out of hand. This theme is at the heart of *Voyage* and explains in part the power the book still has over its readers — especially the younger ones, from whose number military cannon fodder is normally drawn. Also, in fairness to Céline, we should bear in mind the vehemence of his hatred for war as expressed in this novel before taking a critical look at his pamphlets for, as the titles of two of them vividly suggest, he was writing his political tracts to avoid the "massacre" of another war which he thought could produce millions more French "cadavres." Thus, his *Bagatelles pour un massacre* (1937) and *Ecole des cadavres* (1938) refer to his fear of another war — a fear shared by the way by many contemporaries of both the left and the right during the thirties.

But there are also other important themes woven into the fabric of *Voyage*. Céline's rejection of the colonial system at a time when the sun still never set on the far-flung possessions of the French Union was categorical. The message of *Voyage* is clear in this regard: blacks and whites would be much better off if the European would only forsake what he took to be his civilizing mission in Africa and elsewhere, for it contributed ultimately to the well-being of nobody. Céline was also in the vanguard of those writers who brought things American into the modern French novel. His experiences in New York and Detroit, his descriptions of life in these cities with their emphasis on the use of machines to get things done, his praise of the beauty of American women, his recognition of the common sense of the American people and his criticism of life on the assembly line, are among the first signs that the United States — its people, its values, and its way of life — were about to enter the mainstream of French literature.

Finally, there is also an undercurrent of tenderness and human compassion in *Voyage*. The pages mentioned above in which Bardamu talks of Alcide, Molly, and Bébert, not to mention Madame Henrouille, offer examples of occasions where the overall darkness is illuminated by snatches of light that warm the reader and help him find his way, with Bardamu, to the end of his journey. Ultimately, then, we see *Voyage* as a guardedly positive statement on the human condition in the twentieth century. Céline, writing in the "postwar" period of the late twenties and early thirties, living amidst the materialism of a de-Christianized working class, and having had no religious formation himself beyond the rituals of baptism and first communion,[45] was trying to press out of the clay of experience some reason for a modern youth who had been lucky enough to escape death in the insanity of World War I to go on living. The reasons he ultimately gives are free of illusions and they are the best he can find. They are also, in our view, those reasons that keep modern man (who for the most part no longer accepts the notion of a saving God who can confer meaning on both life and death) going about his daily tasks. In a word, one cannot put down *Voyage* without sensing that in the end Céline was convinced that life was still somehow better than death.

Voyage is surely one of those works that we can place in the main current of modernist literature in this century, for most of the themes and techniques we generally associate with modernism are to be found in it. In its portrayal of reality as essentially what the first person hero apprehends it to be and in the revolutionary use of language, *Voyage* is an emminently modernist work. But beyond the completely new use of language, the insertion of everyday speech into the French novel, there is also the question of the overall relationship betwen the *fond* of *Voyage* — that is, the meaning or message that it seeks to communicate — and its *forme* — the way in which the work is structured. To Céline, despite what some critics have said about the novel's seemingly arbitrary conclusion, *fond* and *forme* are intimately linked in this novel, which is divided, as mentioned above, into two parts. The first part, much shorter than the second, ends with Bardamu being a patient in an asylum, and the second finds him the director of one. In both sections he starts with a fresh slate, experiences the worlds of violence, eroticism, travel, and the day to day illusions and depressions of existence, and in both sections he ultimately finds his place only among the insane. In the first part he is put there by society, but in the second part he voluntarily chooses this form of symbolic exile from society. Although *Voyage* is often called "picaresque," and this despite Céline's warning at the very beginning of the work that the journey involved is "entirely imaginary," we feel that this word unfortunately implies mindless or aimless flight when what is involved, on the contrary, is a constant return on the part of Bardamu to society in an attempt to find his place in it.

The structure of the novel helps to elucidate our interpretation of it.[46] The novel begins and ends in Paris, on the right bank, in the vicinity of the place Clichy. The first and second parts of the novel are each divided into four sections in the following way. Part one has its action take place first in Paris, then in the army at war, next in Paris after Bardamu is wounded, and finally in the asylum at Bicêtre. The second part of the novel develops the action of the first part and expands it while always seeming to point back to it. In the first section of the second part of the novel Bardamu has been turned loose from the asylum on his own, but now that he has experienced the war he is no longer the same naive youth he was before he ran off and enlisted. Next, when he goes off first to Africa and then to America, Céline goes out of his way to point out to the reader that the experiences he had had in these two places were like the ones he had known during the war. The third section of part two, just like the third section of part one, brings Bardamu back to the Paris area (including a side trip to Toulouse which, like the trip to the parc Saint Cloud in the corresponding section of part one, makes him more lucid), and from here he will enter the asylum at Vigny-sur-Seine which corresponds to the sojourn at Bicêtre in part one. This structure, in its simplest form, looks something like this:

Paris   Paris

War   Africa — America

Paris — parc Saint-Cloud   Paris — Rancy — Toulouse

Asylum — Bicêtre   Asylum — Vigny-sur-Seine

The ultimate meaning of this structure, hidden beneath the surface but obviously worked out by Céline in great detail, is to make clear to us by the end of the novel the choices that Bardamu has made. He has not committed suicide, but neither has he hade his truce with society. A state of tension continues to exist as the novel ends. But Bardamu, unlike Robinson, is still very much alive and is literally moving forward at the end of the book.

   Another modernist theme, according to which the novelist writes for no other reason than to see life and the world more clearly himself, also comes through strongly in *Voyage*. Bardamu is still a stranger to society by the end of the novel, but he is no longer a stranger to himself. For this reason the ending of *Voyage* is not an arbitrary one. The story does not just break off, as some readers of *Voyage* have suggested. On the contrary, it ends because the hero has come to the end of his own night — the night of self-understanding. Of course night also represents death for Céline; and in fact Robinson is dead by now, and with him a possible course of action — pursuit of a selfish life based on complete independence of others — has been put to rest. Bardamu himself has lucidly and pessimistically concluded that the world is mad, but, given the choice between suicide and accommodation to society, he takes a middle road by choosing to live among the insane. But he opts for life nonetheless, and where there is life there is, even for Bardamu with his past history of failure and disillusionment, still hope.

VI   L'Eglise (The Church)

With Céline's reputation assured by the publication and success of *Voyage*, his editor, while waiting for him to write another novel, looked around for something else to publish. Literature, no matter how highly one idealizes the state in which it should exist, is still a creature of the marketplace in our day, and publishers are usually anxious to capitalize to the utmost on any hot literary property they happen to fall upon. In the case of Céline therefore, the author and publisher agreed to bring out the text of a play that Céline had actually written before he wrote *Voyage*. The work, entitled *L'Eglise*, is a "comédie" in five acts that lacks not only unity but also that quintessential something without which no play can hope to succeed: a sense of dramatic presence, the ability to inspire in the spectator (or reader) the feeling that something is happening, even if the action is taking place inside the characters. Here, however, *L'Eglise* succeeds only in putting one to sleep. In fact, it is so boring, so poorly constructed, and so lacking in dramatic interest that it ought not even be mentioned. But since the play is part of the Céline legend,[47] that is, the legend created by the political personality, and since it also bears a special relationship to *Voyage*, a few words are in order.

Critics have tended generally to avoid mentioning the play in detail, contenting themselves with pointing out, as we have, that it is a poor play that rambles on and that it ought not be produced. In fact, when Céline tried to have it produced after the success of *Voyage*, it was refused by a Parisian director, and the only time it was produced during his own lifetime was by a troop of amateurs in Lyons. It ran for only one performance, and its merits are so slight that it deserves no more than this. It has been produced once in recent times, though, by the Théâtre de la Plaine in 1973 — and although it was received this time more positively than before, the *animateur* who staged the play — François Joxe — did not meet with any overwhelming public interest. No amount of interest or enthusiasm can bring a dead work to life.[48]

Unfortunately, as is often the case with Céline, one gets the impression from reading critics that he was already writing like a fascist when, in the late twenties (probably 1928), he put this play together. Erika Ostrovsky, for instance, sees the play as an "antisemitic satire,"[49] while Bettina Knapp, in her at times factually unreliable book on Céline, gets so carried away by the third act of the play in her description of the work that she forgets to mention the last two acts. Instead, she rambles on to the effect that here "the artist has vanished and been replaced by a man spewing hate."[50] Allen Thiher, on the contrary, seems to think that the play might better be considered as a "parody of anti-Semitism."[51] Given this contradiction in viewpoint, we shall here briefly describe what this dreary play purports to be about and pinpoint why the question of anti-Semitism arises in discussing it.

The first of the five acts takes place in Africa, and Doctor Bardamu already has his opposite number, Pistil, present here in embryonic form. Pistil is a drinker who has been in the colony too long, and the conversation in this act drags on about the horrors of the climate and the clash of African and French values in the colonized territory. The dialogue states Céline's views on blacks (he generally dislikes them), on colonialism (as we know, he was against it), and on the English (they annoy him almost as much as do Jews). All through this act, during which a ludicrous governor general appears and learns that an American physician, Dr. Gaige, has died, the conversation drags on until, by its end, Clapot, the inspector general, insists that if this young doctor died, it must have been because, just before arriving in a French colony, he passed through an English one. And of course the English, as opposed to the French, are known for neglecting to respect the need for at least minimal sanitary standards in their colonies.

As Act II opens we find Bardamu in New York. He is there to find the wife of Dr. Gaige in order to announce to her the news of her husband's death. Inevitably, she is a dancer and Céline takes advantage of this fact to discourse a bit on dancers' legs (between which of course Bardamu is ever anxious to place himself). Gaige's wife, Elizabeth, and another dancer, Vera Stern, say nothing of much interest, and the two French characters in this act, Marcel, a hairdresser in his midtwenties, and the vapid young Flora Bonjour, are hardly developed at all. At the beginning of the act there is a reference to a certain Max, whom we never see throughout the whole play, who has left the U.S. for France because his papers do not seem to be in order. This reference, it seems to us, prefigures the situation of Robinson who, in *Voyage*, must leave Chicago to return to Paris for a reason similar to Max's departure. But how can we care about Max if we never see him or learn anything more about him? It should be noted, however, that the ship on which Max travels to France is called the *Youpinium* (*Oeuvres*, I, 405), a fact worth pointing out since in French the slang word "youpin" is roughly translatable as "kike" in English. Also of note is the fact that the mindless Flora Bonjour is offered a job as an actress in a musical revue by a "manager" named "Blum" (*Oeuvres*, I, 419-20). If we presume that Blum is a Jew, then we can add further significance to the fact that he wants Flora to play opposite a Chinese fellow in this musical at the Blagwill Follies. Later, in the pamphlets, Céline would equate Jews with mongrelization and with "oriental" characteristics. Here perhaps we have a foreshadowing of that demented vision.

In Act III we have another abrupt change of scene for now Bardamu is in Geneva at the headquarters of the League of Nations where he must report to his superiors about the death of Gaige. The office is run by a Polish Jew named Judenzweck who is assisted by a handful of equally hypocritical characters. Among them, in addition to two Jewish stereotypes named Moïse and Mosaïc, there are other cardboard creatures like the plump Dutchman Van Den Prick, the romantic Hungarian military officer Cravach, a "Scandinavian Idealist," and of course a red-headed Englishman adept at furthering his country's interests at the expense of others (*Oeuvres*, I, 430). The plot of this act is simple. Bardamu was not present at the death of Doctor Gaige and for reasons he did not explain he never took the trouble to perform an autopsy on the corpse after Gaige's death. Therefore he is not sure that the man died of yellow fever. His report on the death of Gaige is thus only one page in length and states only what Bardamu knows to be a fact. Judenzweck, good bureaucrat that he is, has turned this report into a thick volume that says no more nor less than what Bardamu can vouch for, but of course it does so in amplified bureaucratic form.

There is also an incident here in which Céline gives vent to his conviction (voiced repeatedly later in the pamphlets) that Jews and Englishmen usually work well together. In this incident we find Judenzweck at first hypocritically agreeing with Ventrenord, a French military representative, that Gaige first contracted his illness in the *saxon* colony. Then, once Ventrenord has left his office, Judenzweck turns around and assures the representative of the "saxons" that the final report will blame the death of Gaige on the French. Judenzweck also offers his hand to Bardamu in friendship in this scene — the bureaucrat seemingly wanting to take an interest in an operative working under his orders — and asks the young doctor why he ever decided to practice medicine. When Bardamu offers much the same response that Robinson will later give us in *Voyage* for his wanting to become a nurse, and with which Bardamu there will agree (you can protect yourself better against others when they are ill and you are healthy), we can see why Judenzweck will be prompted before the final curtain of this act to drop Bardamu from the League of Nations' payroll. After all, despite Céline's own persecution complex and his dislike for Jews, how can we fault Judenzweck, a Jew, a bureaucrat, and, let us presume, a humanitarian, when he hears Bardamu respond: "Okay, I prefer dealing with sick people. Those who are well are so cruel, so stupid; once they get back on their feet they want to seem so clever that one's every dealing with them is almost right away an unfortunate one. When they're in bed and in pain they leave you alone. Got it?"[52] Finally, despite the fact that Céline specifies in his staging directions that Judenzweck is presumably supposed to look Jewish — that is; thick glasses, big nose, all dressed in black, forever, looking "prudent, trés prudent"[53] — we can say that the play is "anti-Semitic" only if we also state that it is "anticolonial," "anti-British," "anti-modern-life-in-the-United-States," and "antifeminine." Such a parade of epithets does not, to our view, serve the cause of lucid criticism very well. In a word, Céline does express in this play, notably in Act III, but also, as we have pointed out, in Act II, his dislike for Jews, but that does not make the play an anti-Semitic one in the sense that his pamphlets can clearly be called anti-Semitic.

This reader, for example, agrees that Judenzweck acts hypocritically when he says one thing to Ventrenord and then contradicts his given word a few minutes later. But to see the play as anti-Semitic for this reason is to state categorically that a Jew in literature cannot act like other fallible mortals. Judenzweck, although clearly presented as a Jew, stands out no more than do the other various national stereotypes. Furthermore, he is a bureaucrat with all the institutional allegiances that such a position implies. Thus, when he sees to it that Bardamu, at the end of the act, will henceforth cease to exist as far as he is concerned, this dropping of an uncooperative medical man by an organization man is not only logical, given the characterization, but also an act that evokes the sympathy of the reader-spectator. For given what we know of Bardamu so far, Judenzweck is protecting the interests of the League in dropping him. Bardamu thinks too much and is overly critical, and organizations usually try to eliminate such people. Ultimately, in a question like this, we are dealing with a question of degree. This critic does not see *The Merchant of Venice*, for instance, as an anti-Semitic play and deplores the fact that for years it could not be read or played by New York City public school students. There are, however, those who see Shakespeare's play as the work of an anti-Semite. It is probably fair to say that people such as this would probably feel the same way about *L'Eglise*. To our mind though, the term is better saved for use in more clear-cut circumstances. If *L'Eglise* is anti-Semitic then what are *Bagatelles pour un massacre* and *Ecole des cadavres*?

In Act IV, we find Bardamu back in the Paris suburbs. The prototype of Rancy is called here Blabigny-sur-Seine. Pistil, like Robinson, who will work as a *garçon* in a café in *Voyage* after his return from the United States and before his attempted murder of Madame Henrouille, here owns a café that he has bought with a pension he has received for his colonial service. The name of the establishment, "Au Repos des Colonies," indicates this connection. In this scene Céline joins Pistil and Bardamu more closely together than in the earlier scenes for here Bardamu practices medicine right in Pistil's café. Since he has not yet been able to scrape up the money to set up his own office, he treats people right there in public view. He is also dragging a child along with him, a little black boy who had appeared in Act II (where he was called Dr. Gaige's illegitimate offspring) and whose paternity is never really made clear. The boy is just about ready for school now and, if anything, he can be taken as the symbol of the psychological hangover, the psychic baggage that Pistil/Bardamu carry about with them as a result of their travels in Africa. Like malaria, which never leaves one who has first contracted it, this little boy, mockingly named Gologolo, will follow Bardamu about and will serve as a reminder throughout this play of the African stage in the hero's journey. Vera Stern, the dancer whom he had met in Act II, is in France now but she leaves to go back to work as a dancer in New York. Before she leaves there are a few words about love between her and Bardamu and one is reminded, just before she leaves, of Bardamu's attachment in *Voyage* to Molly, whom he also claims to have loved. She departs anyway. There is another female in this act, a young invalid who walks with a limp and has a slight hunch on her back. She asks Bardamu for advice about physical therapy which he kindly supplies. Later, in Act V, when she offers herself to him he will not accept.

In the final act of this would-be *comédie*, the action again takes place in the bistro, which by this time has been transformed into a clinic. Robinson, we recall, dies in *Voyage* before the end of the novel. Likewise, his prototype Pistil is dying here from chronic alcoholism. Toward the end of the act, the shortest one in the play, Elizabeth Gaige appears and begins a kind of rapid, Ginger Rogers style dance number while taking off her clothes to the music of a song entitled "No More Worries." A few pages before Elizabeth's appearance, Bardamu had issued his final message, the dark message that haunted Céline his whole life — namely, that "the saddest thing of all, listen to me, is death ... love, is the fear of death."[54] Given this negative remark, this assertion that man's most noble gesture, the gift of self to another, is ultimately and completely sullied by the fear of death, one can finally interpret Elizabeth's appearance as a kind of provisional *deus ex machina*. Céline seems to be saying in effect that life is a journey ending in a senseless death. But if, along the way, we can for a few fleeting instances forget this horror through music, and especially dance — in which the beauty of the human body lifts him up, out, and away from this sad vision — then he will be able to say that he has enjoyed happiness.

The question arises as to what Céline might have meant by giving the title *L'Eglise* to this hodgepodge of dramatic action. It seems to us that the most sensible way to interpret the title is to take the word at its root value in Greek, — that is, the sense of assembly or community that the Greek word *ekklesia* possesses. And when we enlarge this notion of community to embrace the whole of mankind, we see that Céline is aiming his barb at no less a target than man and his nature, and in fact at all of humanity. Whether in Africa, the New World, Geneva, that enlightened capital of international peace and finance, or in the dreary suburban hole known as Blabigny-sur-Seine, he is forever within the confines of that "église" where man has his way, a way that leads inevitably to death. Another less likely, but nonetheless possible, interpretation of the title could take the "church" of the title to mean that group of individuals that would later be attacked in the pamphlets: freemasons, Englishmen, Jews, marxists, liberals, and idealists.

In conclusion, we have chosen to mention this play only after first discussing the novel of which it is a prefigurement, for the simple reason that the play cannot really be taken as an important work of art in its own right. In the final analysis *L'Eglise* has meaning for us only in that it was written by a novelist of great ability — who was not, we must add, endowed as a playwright. Beyond that, the work is of interest only in so far as it illustrates a kind of *Ur-Voyage*, a preliminary, tentative attempt by Céline to come to grips with his own personal demons; and the distance traversed from this poor play to *Voyage* is a great one indeed. Finally, since Céline was later to display an ugly, distasteful, and unjustified hatred of Jews, we get the earliest glimpses in *L'Eglise* of that much-discussed side of his character.

CHAPTER 3

The Mature Style

I Ferdinand's Adolescence: Mort à crédit

THE narrator of *Mort à crédit* seems to be an older Ferdinand who is looking back on his past. Before he begins his story, though, he tells us a few things about himself: for instance, that he is a doctor currently employed in a clinic called "the Linuty Foundation"; that he is an insomniac, "If I had always slept properly, I'd never have written a line";[1] and that he has already enjoyed enough sexual pleasure in life to be able to face death, "I'd have almost enough put by to settle my accounts with death ... I had my esthetic savings. What marvelous ass I'd enjoyed, I've got to admit it, as luminous as light. I had tasted of the Infinite." These revelations at the beginning of the novel establish the identity of the narrator quite faithfully. He is a crank who thinks of nothing but himself. The next five hundred pages or so are an elaboration of how this rather unpleasant person would have you believe he spent his youth.

Whereas in *Voyage* Céline had only occasionally used "les trois points," or the stylistic technique of breaking sentences into smaller units separated by three dots, here in *Mort* we find this technique in evidence from the outset. Also, whereas from a structural point of view *Voyage* can be called a traditional realistic novel that tells a story in chronological order from beginning to end with much detail that reminds us that we are almost always in the middle of a concrete world recognizable to all, in *Mort* no such universe is created for us. While *Voyage* retains some of the outer trappings of a realist novel (basically an expressionist work),[3] *Mort* is more obviously expressionist in tone.[4] Here, from the opening pages, he is expressing feelings, dreams, hallucinations, and periods of delirium, and is switching back and forth in time as the

whim of his inspiration dictates. For this reason no detailed
systematic notion can be clearly communicated of what this novel
"is about" in the same way that we were able to do with *Voyage*.
Instead, we shall have to offer a brief resumé of the main points of
the narrative and then backtrack to cover those points that
illustrate major themes and stylistic strategies in the novel.

We recall that Ferdinand Bardamu would lapse into delirium at
certain times during narrative events of *Voyage*, when Robinson
was beyond reach. Here, in the overture or prelude to *Mort*, or
about the first thirty pages of the novel, Céline serves notice on his
reader that this device, which both represents an escape from
reality for the protagonist and a means of disposing of his past, is
to be used in a more developed and sophisticated manner in *Mort*.
The narrator tells us that his cousin is a doctor like himself and then
recalls how he used to tell a fairy tale of his own invention to this
cousin when they were children. The fairy tale is the story of King
Krogold, a seemingly medieval warrior of some kind who, betrayed
by his enemy, Gwendor, defeats the latter in battle and then takes
vengeance on his subjects. In a word, this is the cruel world of
senseless bloodshed in which, for reasons never made clear, the
poor, the humble, and the innocent are destroyed for something
they never did and for reasons they cannot understand. The themes
of death, betrayal, and vengeance, important in the novel itself, are
presented in embryonic form in this "legend."

But whereas in *Voyage* this type of message, so central to
Céline's vision of life, was conveyed in a realistic mode, the means
of communication here is a highly individualized, personal, and
subjective one. Thus our term "expressionist" novel. Ferdinand
will not be asked to go out and kill Germans the way Bardamu was
ordered to do; instead we get the impression through the recurrence
throughout the novel of little bits of the tale — as it mounts to the
surface of the older narrator's consciousness — of the inevitable
recurrence of war and death or mindless, unreasonable killing as a
way of life. But abruptly the dream is broken off and a link is made
with another thread of continuity that *Mort* has with *Voyage*. The
narrator has had trouble with people circulating rumors about him.
A proletarian girl named Mireille, who had already had seven
different factory jobs by the time she was sixteen, wants the doctor,
or anybody, to marry her. Like Madelon in *Voyage*, marriage is the
way to security for her, the only hope of elevating herself out of

poverty. Ferdinand waits in hiding for her, to talk to her on her way home. Jumping out from his hiding place he greets her with a kick that sends her sprawling. Then they decide to go for a walk and talk things over. But here the first of several delirium or hallucination scenes begins. In the midst of the Bois de Boulogne, he gives her a slap to remind her not to spread rumors about him and then a hallucinatory vision ensues in which thousands of people attack and beat each other as they run from the Bois de Boulogne to the Arch of Triumph where 25,000 policemen finally put an end to the masochistic orgy. The scene ends abruptly and Ferdinand wakes up at home in a sweat. He has had a bad dream.

After this opening section, which is seen by some as a pastiche by Céline of the "supposedly reclining position of the Proustian narrator, [for] as Dr. Ferdinand recollects his childhood memories, he lies sick in bed, periodically vomiting,"[5] we proceed to the resurrection of Ferdinand's grim past. He grows up in a glass encased passage in Paris, called in the novel the passage des Bérésinas, which in *Voyage* was known for the prostitutes who worked there. The family consists of Ferdinand; his father, a low at the heels insurance man who has never made much of himself despite his diploma in literature; and his mother, Clémence, who runs a lace shop on the ground floor of their place, located downstairs from the family's cramped living quarters above. While his father would have liked to be a sailor and loved ships, but had never indulged this inclination, his mother is a hard-nosed business person who devotes all her energy to her small but doomed lace shop, for the larger department stores are slowly driving her out of business. Furthermore, the poor woman walks with a limp, but despite her disability she is able to hobble about the city to make her calls. At home, when the members of the family are not battling with each other, they cannot even really enjoy the taste of decent food to alleviate their personal frustrations, for the odor of anything but noodles would contaminate the lace she has stored away in the shop. Thus Ferdinand eats hardly anything but noodles, beans, or bread soup.

The neighbors in the passage do not make life much easier either. Madame Méhon, who lives right across from Ferdinand's family, is always trying to start a fight with them, and the families up the way a bit, the De Caravals and the Pérouquières, are hardly the friendliest of neighbors. In addition, for a small businesswoman like Clémence, life is complicated by what she takes to be the necessity of ignoring insult — even when the insult goes so far as to take the form of thievery. When a well-to-do customer from a wealthy neighborhood takes a valuable handkerchief from before her very eyes, neither Ferdinand nor Clémence protests, for to do so might alienate the potential customer. They put up with everything, so it is no wonder that Ferdinand confides that "I just shouldn't have been born."[6]

The fourth member of the *ménage* is grandmother Caroline, Clémence's mother, who dies after about one hundred pages of the novel. The family seems to be genuinely bereaved, but Ferdinand feels that his father was shattered only because there was nobody but himself left to have arguments with. Exaggerated self-interest and an inability to get outside oneself and communicate with others wall these people up within themselves. Another neighbor, Madame Cortilènes, is admired by the young Ferdinand for her beauty and he is even able to catch a glimpse of her shoulders when she comes to his mother's shop for fittings. But beauty only turns Ferdinand senselessly back upon himself, for after each of these fittings, "the moment she left, it never failed, I'd run up to the can on the fourth floor and masturbate strenuously. I'd come down with big rings under my eyes."[7] In fact, when Ferdinand is not vomiting, he is usually masturbating, or defecating in his pants, as he does, for instance, on the day he graduates from primary school. Ferdinand feels impelled to soil whatever is legitimately beautiful or joyful.

The impression fostered in *Voyage* that Robinson/Bardamu were from the lower end of the social scale is continued here, for as soon as Ferdinand finishes primary school, he must begin hunting for a job. Not long after taking his first position as a stockboy he is fired, and then his second job, working for the jeweler Gorloge, ends when he loses a precious stone after having been seduced by Gorloge's wife.[8] But in spite of these commercial setbacks, his parents still try to do their utmost to push their son along the road to maturity. Their dream, given their social background, is entirely legitimate and logical. They want their son to succeed in the business world some day and so they make a financial sacrifice and send him off to school in England where, it is hoped, he will learn English.

Before Ferdinand even sets foot in Meanwell College, he has an erotic encounter with a local girl named Gwendoline and leaves her almost as fast as he meets her. Then once he arrives at the school, he decides that he is not going to speak either English or French, and so for three months he does his best to avoid learning anything. His most notable acquaintance at the school is Jongkind, a drooling idiot looked after by the headmaster's wife Nora, who devotes herself tirelessly to the financial survival of her husband's ridiculous prep school: "For Nora the idiot was an awful nuisance, she had every reason to be exhausted at the end of the afternoon. ... Just wiping his nose, taking him to pee, keeping him from getting run over, from swallowing everything in sight ... it was really a rotten chore. ..." [9] Nora finally takes out her frustrations in a carnal attack on Ferdinand. They copulate and part ways and after eight months away from home the boy comes back to Paris.

After hanging around his parents' home for some time waiting for something to happen (and this period culminates in a brawl with his father during which he almost kills Auguste), he is introduced, thanks to his mother's brother Edouard, to the inventor and con man Courtial des Pereires. Courtial is the editor and contributor to a popular science magazine of the day, *Genitron*. He is forever in motion — writing, speaking, and doing research of sorts in his role as a kind of Don Quixote of Science. In this role he is served faithfully by Ferdinand, his Sancho Panza. Examples of his work are his experiments with electricity and with a lighter than air balloon named the Enthusiast. After a while, when some of the subscribers to his magazine come around and break up his office in anger at having been bilked, Courtial and Ferdinand are forced to transfer their activities outside the city to the suburb of Montretout. But even there things keep getting worse. Thus they soon leave Montretout behind and buy a piece of property in the countryside where they decide they will start up a farm where youngsters can come and combine work, fun, and instruction in the agricultural arts. When this too turns to failure, Courtial commits suicide. Hardly a perfect man (he had been an inveterate horse player and, according to his wife, indulged in perversions with little girls, exposing himself in the Gare du Nord), his death is greeted by his disciple in a cold, anatomical way. Man, defined at one point in *Voyage* as "arrested putrescence," [10] is no more here than a bag of rotten matter. Courtial's journey is ended, the better now to get rid of him before his remains stink too much. Unemployed again, Ferdinand returns to Paris where he stays with his uncle Edouard. There is no sense in going back to see his parents at this point — they have lost interest in him. His future plans? He will simply join the army, a decision that will take him to the point where the previous novel, *Voyage*, began.

II *Themes and Style in* Mort à crédit

As mentioned above, the stylistic device of the three dots is exploited to the maximum in this novel. Its use is essential to an understanding of Céline's *ars poetica*. To him, the key to fictional creation is transposition, a process that takes place regarding both style and the creation of character. In one of his letters to Milton Hindus, written while in exile in Denmark, Céline describes his technique as follows: he wants to "re-sensitize the language so that it pulses more than it reasons."[11] His use of slang in both of his early novels and his dealing with the seamier aspects of the lives of common, everyday people, were an integral and essential part of his strategy as a novelist. To him the literary language of the thirties was several generations behind the spoken language. Formal written French, to his mind, had lost touch with the reality that it is ultimately supposed to express: the pulsating life of the people who speak the language. In revolt against this state of affairs he thus decided that he had to put spoken language into literature in order to create a form of literary expression that he could be content with.

Still, to put spoken language into writing is a mere trick. And I found it — nobody else. Making spoken words go in literature isn't stenography: you have to change the sentences and rhythms somehow, to distort them — to use an artifice, so that when you read a book, it's as though someone is actually speaking to you. That's brought about by transposing each word, which never seems to be exactly the one you're expecting — but a little surprise. ... The same thing happens as with a stick plunged into water. If you want it to look straight you have to break it slightly — or bend it, you might say. When you put one end in, a normally straight stick looks bent — and the same with language. On the page the liveliest dialogue taken down word for word seems flat, complicated, heavy. ...[12]

But subject matter and characterization are also involved in the creation of a literary world, and to achieve his desired effects in this realm he found that he also had to transpose: "To reproduce the effect of spontaneous spoken life on the page, you have to bend language in every way — in its rhythm and cadence, in its words. A kind of poetry weaves the best spell: the impression, the fascination, the dynamism. Then too, you must choose your subject — not everything can be transposed. You have to lay back the flesh of your subjects — and this means terrible risks. But now you have all my secrets." [13] Whereas the technique of breaking sentences into small pieces separated by three dots is used only sparingly in *Voyage*, the whole of *Mort* is written this way. But to our view the essential rhythms of Céline's prose are identical in the two books, with only the outward sign, the three dots, being more visible in *Mort à crédit*.

Also, although both *Voyage* and *Mort* are autobiographical novels, this question of transposition is usually considered to be much more critical in the latter work than in the former, for in *Mort* the portrait of Ferdinand's parents is so negative that one wonders if the narrator is telling the truth. Were his parents so poor and desperate, did the family members all get along so poorly with each other, and was his father, in particular, such a miserable and disagreeable person? The answers to all of these questions seem to be negative. Available testimony indicates in fact that Céline's father was not all that badly off financially (we even know the amount of his retirement pay),[14] and his mother seems to have been a woman who was tenderly devoted to her son. The family was not genuinely *bourgeois* in character, nor was it a working class family — existing on the contrary in the social no man's land which French sociologists sometimes call an "entre-deux-classes" of lower echelon white collar workers. His parents did, however, manage to send Céline to study both in Germany and in England, a sacrifice on their part that should be recalled, and of course his mother would later stand by him when his political views in the late thirties isolated him even from French fascists.[15]

Beyond the immediate family, we know that transformation also takes place both with respect to Meanwell College and the characters presented there, and regarding the obsessed inventor Courtial des Pereires. This character, for instance, seems to be based on a real life person named Raoul Marquis, for whom Céline worked for several months during 1918 between his return from the

Cameroons and his departure for Rennes. Marquis, under the name of Henry de Graffigny, published a magazine named *Eurêka* (transposed to *Genitron*) which indulged in the same kind of popular science speculation that we find in *Mort*. [16] Graffigny, who was apparently consumed by "le démon de l'invention," [17] is caricatured by Céline, who takes the recognizable character traits of his model and blows them out of proportion in order to get the desired effect. Thus, many of these characters, especially the most important ones, are based on people Céline actually knew at some time in his life, and it is for this reason that the reader would be ill-advised to think that one can for a moment cease to distinguish between the author on the one hand and his narrator-protagonist on the other. Their connections are deeply seated and fundamental, but the biographies of Ferdinand and of Bardamu/Robinson should not be confused with Céline's.

Beyond the questions of the three dots and of the transposition of language and subject matter, there is the matter of the periodic eruption of delirium and of hallucination in this novel. These eruptions go beyond the ones in *Voyage*, alluded to above, in which Bardamu is transported in a slave galley from Africa to New York, and in which, asleep in Tania's bed, he relives past experiences, both by the vividness of physical, naturalistic detail and by the gratuitous hallucinatory exaggeration of it all.

There are several such scenes in the book, the most celebrated of which is probably the one in which Ferdinand and his parents enjoy their only real respite from the boredom and tedium of their existence when they take a brief trip to Dieppe. There they decide for the fun of it to take a boat trip over to England, and at this point Céline takes advantage of the situation to transpose everything.[18] But when he goes into this delirious state before his reader's eyes and paints a highly exaggerated picture of people getting seasick all over each other, it is well to recall that a sub-stratum of lived experience is usually ultimately at the base of the verbal explosion. To him, "if a thing doesn't sing, the soul doesn't know it exists. To hell with reality! I want to die in music, not in reason or in prose. People don't deserve the restraint we show by not going into delirium in front of them." [19] Finally, the use of the delirium technique can also be found at other points in *Mort*, notably in a scene on the dock in Folkstone, in a scene describing Nora and Ferdinand in bed together, and in the instance of a visit to his mother's shop by a transposed lady customer.

Also, for the remainder of his career as a novelist, Céline would use delirium as a conscious technique. Its use in *Mort*, as we remarked above, is different from its use in *Voyage*, however, for here Céline is much more certain of his verbal powers. To define it more precisely, the formula put together by Michel Beaujour is perhaps the best one available. He writes:

Delirium is therefore ambivalent. For it is, at the same time, both that which permits one to live in spite of everything, and an integral part of human unhappiness since the world is the totality of interacting deliriums. ... This is why insane asylums play such a role in *Voyage*: blessed places where real crazy people, protected from the agitated world of more murderous deliriums, can fully enjoy their divagations among themselves. The real catastrophe, always at hand, is the end of the delirious state, the loss of total illusion.[20]

To Beaujour, *Mort* is a constellation of deliriums in which each person is essentially happy in his own little world except the narrator. And when Courtial commits suicide at the end of the novel, it is because he is no longer able to entertain his own "délire."

Another aspect of Céline's use of delirium in his novels that has not been studied fully to date is the debt he owes to Léon Daudet, whose book *Le Rêve éveillé* (*The Waking Dream*),[21] seems to have largely influenced Céline. To Daudet, the problem from antiquity onward was that all those who had studied the problem of dreams, from Lucretius to Freud and Havelock Ellis, had presumed that dreams only occurred in a sleeping state. He tried to show, however, that in fact the human being also dreams while he is awake and that the "waking dream is, in man, the raw material of imagination, the reservoir into which the imagination constantly (and, in a normal state, freely) digs."[22] The human will is also involved in this process, for by freely allowing the dream state to rise to the surface of consciousness through a voluntary suspension of the rational faculties, man is able to clearly see his waking dream. As Colin Nettelbeck has pointed out,[23] Céline had probably read *Le Rêve éveillé* by the time he was at work on *Mort*, for he seems to refer to Daudet in his 1933 speech "Hommage à Zola."[24] He clearly states in *Bagatelles pour un massacre* that he owed much to Daudet's book,[25] but we cannot be sure how early he had read it.

In any case, whereas the dream-delirium technique of *Voyage* is essentially a tool used by Bardamu to elude an unpleasant reality, it becomes in *Mort* a deliberately conscious way of looking at the world.

As for the Legend of King Krogold, also mentioned above, critics differ on its interpretation. To Allen Thiher, for instance, the legend represents Céline's attempt to show his "refusal of heroic poetry." [26] "No one at any age is very much interested in heroic poetry," [27] "not even children, he says, and Céline wants to make it clear through the telling of this story (to which listeners usually do not pay attention) that he has no intention of telling such tales. And yet, as Colin Nettelbeck convincingly argues, the King Krogold story is important to the novel in another way; for "... the themes of the legend — death, betrayal, vengeance — although they are major themes in the novel, are less relevant than the fact that Céline is casting an image of the novelist as a teller of tales that ennoble and transcend reality and elevate the spirit of the listener by their poetic vision." [28] This point is important, for it indicates the view that Céline, who would later refer to himself in the Hindus correspondence as a "daydreamer" and a "bard," [29] had of himself. "I'm first of all a Celt — *daydreamer, bard,*" he wrote to Milton Hindus. "I can turn out legends like taking a leak — with disgusting ease. Scenarios, ballets — anything you like — while I'm talking alone. That's my real talent. I harnessed it to realism because I hate man's wickedness so much; because I love combat. But actually, legends are my music. And I don't get them from libraries or from Chinese folklore like all our neo-bards — but entirely from my own making, from my own head." [30]

Having started from an autobiographical point of view in *Voyage*, he seems to have wanted to objectify his novels as much as possible and at the same time to link himself with one of the most ancient forms of French literature, that oral form that flourished in the northwest of France in the early middle ages and which is thought to be at the base of works like the Tristan legend and of the Arthurian material exploited later by writers like Chrétien de Troyes. Once again, Céline affirms his literary ancestry and his basic artistic allegiances. His is not the language of the academic, school-trained writer, but rather of the wandering storyteller. He does not seek his audience among the literati but, hopefully, among the simple and common folk. Thus, starting with *Mort*, he most likely wanted to give his novels a more objective value, as documents of a sort, that could live apart from his own life story. But at the same time the insertion of the legend in this novel — a story that always seems to induce sleep in the listener — probably indicates that Céline realized full well that the "matière," or subject matter, he knew best was himself. *That*, at least, he could make interesting. Indeed, *Voyage* can be read as nothing more than a work of autoanalysis.

Critical opinion is divided on whether *Voyage* or *Mort* is the better of Céline's first two novels. At the time of their composition in the thirties, critics generally responded positively to *Voyage*, and in fact the subsequent silence that Céline kept after the publication of that book and the great controversy that it aroused was such that some of the critics who hailed the first book expressed disappointment at the second. René Lalou, for instance, saw *Mort* as "monotonous" and went on: "Such a bet against humanity can only stand up for seven hundred pages by using artifice."[31] On balance, however, the verbal pyrotechnics of *Mort à crédit* were so powerful and evident that critical reception on the whole was positive. For this reader, however, *Mort*, no matter how visible the presence of Céline's poetic genius is in the text, still lags. Like *Voyage*, it can be divided into two parts, the first part ending just about midway through the text, with Ferdinand's battle with his father, and the second part commencing with Uncle Edouard's putting the youth in touch with Courtial. The movement in the first part of *Mort* takes place especially in time, with Ferdinand shuffling his memories before our eyes like so many cards in his deck of tricks, while the second part is characterized by the hero's remaining more or less in one place instead of moving about constantly.

How then do we find that *Mort* lags in comparison to *Voyage*? The first and most important reason for this failure in *Mort* is that it becomes obvious after reading not too far along that the hero is going nowhere. Not that social or spiritual redemption is an absolute prerequisite for a *Bildungsroman* — which is what this novel is, despite the totally negative emphasis on the hero's formation. But readers are human and attention must needs waver when it becomes evident — and this is the case after several hundred pages — that what the novelist is doing is using tricks of language and incident to patch together a story that otherwise does not really hold together.

In a word, one is not compelled — as this reader has been for instance each time he has read *Voyage* — to stay with *Mort* and see it through to the end. The atmosphere is, to put it mildly, grim; and after seemingly endless scenes of nausea, masturbation, and paranoia on the part of the hero — who is also an almost perfectly unlikable youth who seems to do everything he can to turn others against him — and of spitefulness, pettiness, envy, jealousy, madness, and perversion on the part of the other characters, one grows tired. Céline cannot be faulted for not having created a world in this novel. He has done that. But the novel can only be said to be successful when the reader desires to gain entry into that world or, better still, when he, once he has set foot therein, has the courage and the desire to keep pushing forward. After several rereadings of *Mort* at widely spaced intervals, this has been the experience of this reader. *Mort à crédit*, despite its power and the evident genius of its creator, ultimately fails to sustain interest. It is probably Céline's funniest book, but even there one laughs so hard at Céline's most successful scenes that one comes close to feeling sick.

III   The Life and Work of Semmelweis

La Vie et l'oeuvre de Philippe-Ignace Semmelweis (*The Life and Work of Semmelweis*) was originally published in 1924.[32] But after the success of Céline the novelist, this work, like *L'Eglise*, was taken out of the closet and republished under the name of Céline.[33] Dr. Destouches was becoming less and less the dominant half of Céline's personality at this time, and the writer with literary ambitions and financial aspirations was gradually overshadowing him. The life and work of Semmelweis, as far as Céline is concerned, are one organic whole. For the devotion of the Hungarian pathologist to his work was so complete, and his eschewing of virtually any other interest in life in order to pursue his professional career was so total, that his work literally consumed his life. In fact it lead directly to his early death.

The text of this work is rather brief, especially by Céline's standards,[34] but if one reads the thesis after having read *Voyage* and *Mort* one has the sensation, much like that felt in reading *L'Eglise*, of discovering an early, tentative working out of themes and questions that would later come to full bloom in *Voyage*. Céline's approach here is forthright and, as in *Voyage*, essentially chronological. After a brief seven page introductory chapter that indicts the French Revolution for the senseless killing that took place during that period in French history, and during which the masses mindlessly "rushed onward to the conquest of an Ideal,"[35] he implies that Europe was saved when "... Napoleon seized Europe and, for good or evil, held it for fifteen years."[36] It was at this time, ever so slowly, that the Romantic era dawned on Europe and the masses began to adore peace just as, fifteen years earlier, they had adored death. Finally, says Céline, it was toward the end of this epoch of convalescence that Semmelweis was born in Budapest, the fourth son of a grocer, in the summer of 1818.

Semmelweis's life story is told simply but powerfully. The biography itself is so strong by itself that there is no need to embellish it with lofty prose, and thus Céline avoids such an approach. He does however allow himself to stop upon occasion to state to his reader his own ideas on the personality of Semmelweis and what his life, in retrospect, should mean to us; but beyond this, the narrative is lean and vibrant. In the introduction to the work Céline illustrates what he takes to be the ultimate meaning of Semmelweis's life when he tells us that "it demonstrates for us the danger of too much goodwill toward men. That is an old lesson that remains forever young."[37]

After receiving his secondary school training in Budapest, young Semmelweis was sent off to Vienna by his father in 1837 to learn law. Before too long, however, he realized that he had no interest in law and switched instead to medicine. Within a short space of time he became the disciple of a brilliantly erudite medical practitioner, a Doctor Skoda, who would henceforth stand by Semmelweis through difficult times. By 1844 he finished his medical degree and two years later received the appointment he sought as a specialist in obstetrics at the Vienna General Hospital, where he was named to begin work on February 27, 1846, as an assistant to a Doctor Klin, who directed one of the hospital's two obstetric clinics.

Semmelweis's problems began soon thereafter when he came to realize that there was a substantial difference between the death rates among women from puerperal fever (an infection of the uterine lining usually caused by unsanitary conditions at childbirth), in the First Clinic directed by Klin and in the Second Clinic directed by a Doctor Bartch. In Klin's clinic the death rate could often go well over fifty percent and it reached as high, one month, as ninety-six percent. In Bartch's clinic on the other hand, the mortality rate never came near the fifty percent figure and was usually much lower. Semmelweis suspected that the reason for the different death rates had something to do with the fact that in Klin's pavilion medical students performed the deliveries, whereas in Bartch's this work was performed by midwives. When he suggested that Bartch and Klin trade staffs for a while, with the medical students going over to work for Bartch and the midwives to Klin, the high mortality rate followed the students. In fact, things became so intolerable for Bartch that he soon sent the students back where they had come from. By this time, Semmelweis was certain that the students played an important role in the etiology of the disease but he still could not specify what that role was. Among his colleagues, that is, among those who were willing to join him in confronting the facts, the shared opinion seems to have been that the higher rate among the students was caused by the fact that the students were less gentle in their work than the midwives, and therefore "their clumsiness, must be the real cause of the fatal inflammation."[38] And as Céline hastens to concede, for he wants to be fair to Semmelweis's enemies, this attitude should not surprise us for in those days it was firmly believed that inflammation was the basic factor in the etiology of puerperal fever.

But Semmelweis was not content with this kind of explanation, and in his zeal he "cut himself off from everyday life, he ignored the outside world, he no longer lived except in the fury of his work."[39] He was on the track of the cause of the disease and was sure he had found its cause when he explained to Klin and others that in following every coming and going of the medical students he had come to the conclusion that they were spreading the disease themselves. Often coming straight from dissections of cadavers to the delivery rooms, they were bringing the disease on their soiled fingers. To counteract this contagion, Semmelweis suggested that these students thoroughly wash their hands before they engage in any work at all in parturition. But routine and ingrained habit turned out to be Semmelweis's enemy, for the students found it too much of a bother to wash. When Semmelweis flew into a rage at their refusal to cooperate, he furnished the pretense that Klin had been waiting for. The latter fired him on October 20, 1846, only

eight months after he had begun working at the hospital. Semmelweis, on the point of making a great discovery, was still but
twenty-eight years old and already professionally discredited.

For the next three years or so Semmelweis withdrew from active
practice. He travelled to Venice for a while and soon after his
return the revolutionary strife of 1848 gripped the country. Finally,
in 1849, he pulled himself together and went back to work in obstetrics at the Saint-Rochus Hospital in Budapest under a Doctor
Birly who hired him only on the condition that he not say anything
to the medical students about washing their hands. Anyway, as
Birly was to hasten to add, washing one's hands in those awful
chlorine solutions would not help prevent the disease anyway, for
to him the problems at Klin's ward had been caused by the fact that
"Klin did not prescribe regular purges for his lying-in patients."[40]
Semmelweis accepted the position and agreed to keep his mouth
closed, but this did not mean that he had abandoned his one obsession: to conquer puerperal fever and discover its cause. Thus he
quietly began the composition of his major work, *The Etiology of
Puerperal Fever.*[41]

For the next four years Semmelweis wrote of his prior experiences in the Vienna hospital with Klin and then, when Birly
died in 1856, he was named as his successor. By this time ten years
had passed since his dismissal by Klin. The long years of silence
seem to have indicated to most of his colleagues that he had kept
still because he recognized that he had been mistaken. Thus when
he published añ "Open Letter to all Professors of Obstetrics," in
which he accused all those who disagreed with him of being
"assassins," and "criminals," declaring "so I call all those who
have defied the rules I prescribed to combat puerperal fever," [42] it
was obvious that Semmelweis was as single-minded as ever regarding this terrible disease.

Only Dr. Arneth, a young obstetrician, rallied strongly to his
cause. Arneth, thinking that Paris was the center of medical
learning of the day and a place where unprejudiced and open minds
would listen to Semmelweis's findings, decided to attend a series of
meetings at the French Academy of Medicine during the summer of
1858. His hope was to convince others of the validity of Semmelweis's conclusions. Unfortunately, when he returned and had to
tell Semmelweis that nobody there took him seriously, he himself
was able to tell the older man that he was resigned for the time

being to the fact that the medical world was just not yet ready to accept such advanced ideas. As Céline writes: "Arneth remained reasonable; Semmelweis could be so no longer. To calculate, to foresee, to wait seemed especially now only forms of impossible tyranny to his now bewildered mind." [43]

Semmelweis could no longer accept the refusal of his ideas by his medical colleagues and so as a result he began to lose his mind, lapsing into frightful states of delirium and hallucination. Finally a delegation of his colleagues convinced him to resign his duties but on the very afternoon of the day he accepted this retirement,

he was seen rushing through the streets, pursued by the mob of his imaginary enemies. Howling, with hands ripping open his shirt, he burst into the anatomical amphitheater of the Medical Faculty. A cadaver lay there on the marble, stretched out, ready for a demonstration in dissection. Semmelweis seized a scalpel, pushed himself through the circle of medical students, thrusting aside several chairs, and thus came nearer to the slab. He punctured the skin of the cadaver, shoved the scalpel deep into the putrid tissues before anyone realized what he was doing. He cut the muscles away in strips, hurled them far behind him. ... The medical students recognized him, but his attitude was so threatening that no one dared to interrupt him. ... He ... explored with his fingers and the blade together a cavity in the dead body which was oozing with liquefaction. With a gesture more abrupt than before, he cut himself profoundly. ... That wound began to bleed. He shouted. He uttered menaces. He was disarmed at last. A crowd gathered around him. But it was too late ... he had infected himself fatally.

When his old friend and protector Doctor Skoda got news of this event in Vienna, he hurried to Budapest to visit with his former disciple. Quickly he whisked him away from the Hungarian city and brought him back to Vienna. On their arrival on June 23, 1865, Semmelweis was placed in an insane asylum where he died a few weeks later on August 16, 1865. During these last days, says Céline, he was nothing more than a "delirious form." [44] The disease took its time in killing him. First lymphangitis, next peritonitis, then pleurisy, and finally meningitis. At this last stage, "he began to babble out with an endless verbal stream, one interminable reminiscence, in the course of which his cracked head seemed to empty itself of long dead phrases." [46] In this, says Céline, "It was no longer that infernal reconstitution of life on the plane of delirium in which he had acted as the tormented protagonist in the first period of his madness."[47] No, this last phase, for Céline, is much less interesting, for Semmelweis's body by this time was already rotting and thus the quality of the delirium in which his mind raged was not up to that which had prevailed earlier.

Convinced that there is nothing but evil in the hearts of men, Céline empathizes deeply with Semmelweis whom he sees as a genius hounded to death by professional envy, small-mindedness, and numbed intellects and deadened emotions among his colleagues caused by a fear of changing established practice. But although his allegiance to Semmelweis is based in part on recognition of his special genius as a man of science, Céline does not pay him homage solely for his uncommon use of the experimental method, or for the rigor of his exposition in his book on puerperal fever. On the contrary, it is for the emotional stamina of the man that Céline has the greatest respect, for to him "man is a creature of feeling. There are no great creations outside the realm of emotion, and enthusiasm rapidly dries up amongst the majority of men, when they wander far from their dream."[48] Semmelweis was a dreamer as well as a genius and for this reason he ran counter to the rest of humanity. No wonder then that he was driven mad by others and finished in a state of delirium which, unlike the personal deliriums of those who persecuted him, led to death.

In this thesis on Semmelweis we see all the major catchwords of Céline's *oeuvre* already being worked out tentatively in preparation for *Voyage*. Death, delirium, hallucination, the theme of the rebel among men who is hounded unjustly by others, the notion that a genius can be born in the most humble of circumstances and that genius is a function of the emotions and not of the intellect. And finally, overhanging all these ideas we see already expressed here the one central idea that would dominate not only *Voyage* but all of Céline's subsequent work — an idea that is not often given the critical recognition it merits. For although Céline does tell us here that "in the endless march of time, Life is nothing but a delirium, the Truth is Death,"[49] he also assures us that he, like Semmelweis, loves life in a very special way that few are able to share. To both of them, life is ultimately beautiful and marvelous simply as a biological marvel: "In fact, Semmelweis drew life from sources too deep to be understood by other men. He was one of those all too rare, who can love life at its simplest and most beautiful — the mere fact of life itself.''[50] It is surely this basic, deep-seated acceptance of life at the very root of his being that kept Semmelweis going until his mind snapped under the weight of pressure from his professional enemies.

Likewise, it seems that this very same deep, emotional, instinctive attachment to life is what would also keep Céline afloat later on both as a novelist and as a doctor able to face existence every day. He might pour out his distaste for alcoholic proletarians, French politicians, masons, Jews, Englishmen, and even, quite often, humanity in general, but when he contemplated life considered in all its epistemological immediacy, as a sudden revelation of being, as a kind of biological wonder, he always had the same positive reaction. He points out here the beauty that he found in life considered solely as a biological phenomenon without any reference to man or to humanistic values, and during the rest of his life this would be the closest he would ever come to what we might call a ''religious'' sentiment. This deep seated sentimental and nonrational acceptance of life is what would later prevent the fictional Bardamu from committing suicide in order to keep coming back again and again to try to make a fresh start in life.

IV   Casse-Pipe (Kick the Bucket)

The title of this work is translated as literally as possible here. The verb in French ''casser la pipe,'' is usually translated as ''to kick the bucket'' in English, but the English translation does not convey the notion of violence contained in the verb, *casser*. The text, published in its entirety for the first time in the Balland edition of the *Oeuvres*, must be consulted in that edition if one is to have a true impression of its worth.[51] The novel obviously was more substantial at one time than it is now, but we are not sure how far along Céline had gotten on it when he stopped work on it. When he fled Paris in 1944, he left it behind and it was later thrown in the garbage by his political enemies.[52] The fragments, which deal with life in a cavalry unit during peacetime, seem to pick up the narration of Ferdinand's life where *Mort* left off. Céline's main goal in these pages is to poke fun at military life, and we treat this text only in passing since it occupies a minor place in Céline's work.

CHAPTER 4

The Pamphleteer

I Mea Culpa

DEALING with what critics have traditionally referred to as the "pamphlets," which are in fact lengthy, rambling, hate-filled diatribes that each run to between three and four hundred pages, is a difficult matter. This is so because in these works we see Céline at his worst, but at the same time we are afforded an opportunity to peer deep into his subconscious. Thus, while we are revolted at the lies and half truths concocted with regard to the Jews, we do see in reading these works where some of the inspiration for the fictional part of Céline's work — however sick that inspiration might have been — could have come from. The word pamphlet is usually used to refer to three lengthy books that Céline published from 1937 through 1941. The first of these, *Bagatelles pour un massacre* (*Trifles for a Massacre*), came out in 1937 and was followed the next year by *Ecole des cadavres* (*School for Cadavers*). Then, in 1941, after the defeat of France, *Les Beaux draps* (roughly translatable as *A Nice Mess*) appeared. None of these books has ever been translated into English; and in fact during the war they were even banned in Germany, a curious testimony to the hatred that their author shows in these works to just about everybody — not only Jews.

It is only recently that critics have begun to look seriously again at the question of anti-Semitism in Céline's work and of course one cannot even begin to treat this question without coming to grips with the pamphlets.[1] We shall attempt to describe below what these works contain, how their arguments are stated, and why Céline felt impelled to write them at the time he did. But we shall also try to offer a fresh perspective on them in that we see these three works as inextricably linked to an earlier pamphlet entitled *Mea Culpa* that

Céline published shortly after his return from the Soviet Union in 1936.

In this work, the young writer, who had been much praised in leftist intellectual circles for his denunciation of the hollowness and emptiness of *bourgeois* life that one finds in *Voyage* and *Mort*, turned his back on the left and castigated the Soviet Union as one vast prison camp where the worker was being systematically put in chains (whereas in France the ruling class was seen as much less efficient, although no less intentionally cruel, at dehumanizing workers). Céline travelled to Russia at his own expense and under the aegis of no group. This point is important, for in the same year, Gide, Guilloux, Dabit, and other writers of the left also made a similar trip, but theirs was under the banner of the *Association des Ecrivains Révolutionnaires et Anti-Fascistes*, a political alignment that suggests that the Soviets hoped that the fact-finders touring the workers' wonderland would come home with a happy picture of life there.[2] As we know, however, Dabit, perhaps more than all the other people in the group of which he was a member, criticized the Soviet system so much that he did not come back alive. More prudently, Gide kept his mouth closed until he got home at which time he wrote *Retour de l'U.R.S.S.*,[3] a work in which he expressed his own misgivings about life and social justice in the Soviet Union. Other writers also underwent a crisis of doubt about Russia after visiting that land, but, in comparison to them, the denunciation of Russia by Céline is, perhaps predictably, cataclysmic.

Céline never got over his lower middle class desire to achieve some semblance of financial security. We should recall in this regard that when he was asked why he had written *Voyage*, he responded that he needed the money, that he had seen the financial success of Eugène Dabit with *Hotel du Nord*,[4] and that he wanted to do the same thing: write a novel, make enough money to buy his own apartment, and live free of financial worry thereafter. From the very beginning, *Voyage* was a colossal commercial success, in addition to being a *succès d'estime*. The royalties that came flowing into Céline's account were, it seems, systematically accumulated and transported before the war to Denmark where they were put in safekeeping. Céline also earned a good deal in royalties through the success of the Aragon and Elsa Triolet translation of his *Voyage* into Russian. But since the Soviets would not send his royalties out of the country, Céline was forced, if he wanted to enjoy the

Russian fruits of his labor, to travel to Russia to do so. His trip did not last long, taking only about two months during the summer of 1936, and like any Westerner visiting Russia in those days he was closely followed. The Soviets assigned an interpreter, a certain Nathalie, to Céline and it was her task not only to show him about the country but also to report on his activities and observations.

Mea Culpa[5] is significant, especially in relation to the pamphlets that were to follow, in that we already find in this work some of the obsessions that were to cloud Céline's mind later on. The only difference is that it is Communists who are the villians in *Mea Culpa*, not Jews. In fact, if Jews are barely even mentioned in *Mea Culpa*, it seems to be because Céline had not yet made the complete connection in his mind between Jews and Communists. He would do so in the very near future, in fact before the publication of *Bagatelles*, but at this time, in late 1936 while writing *Mea Culpa*, he sees the evil in the world as something that is inherent in man, an evil that the Communists in their arrogance think they can make disappear through the process of social engineering.

When one talks of any of these works, the reader should bear in mind that they are not classically organized, clearly reasoned pieces of rhetoric. They are rhetorical, to be sure, but it is in the Célinesque mode that the rhetoric operates. Irony, invective, *ad hominem* assaults, lies, and distortions bubble up and slap the reader or the object of the argument in the face, then fizzle and subside while other arguments, observations, and outraged cries do battle with each other for the reader's attention on succeeding pages. In other words, one comes away from this, Céline's first pamphlet, with much the same feeling one will get from the next three: one is impressed at the agility of the hard-hitting, body-punching prose that destroys an adversary before he can even defend himself and dazzles the reader with its speed and pacing at the same time. But if he achieves his end, Céline also sacrifices a steady line of development to the argument. Classical organization and clear exposition, Mediterranean traits which Céline rejected completely, are here replaced by Céline's would-be Breton, Celtic style, which is seemingly unpolished, primitive, and disorganized. It is closer to what Céline saw as the native French kind of in- spiration, the kind that must have animated the minds of the an- cient Gauls, before the Romans brought them "civilization," with their stifling system of classical education (based on imitation, not inspiration) and their racially inferior mixed blood population (already contaminated with Afro-Asian blood lines, of which he considered the Jews to be the prime example). But here we are getting ahead of ourselves and anticipating the later pamphlets.

If there is no formal organized architecture to *Mea Culpa*, there is nonetheless a bitter diatribe against Communism contained in its pages. In resumé, the less than forty pages of this pamphlet argue as follows. The *bourgeoisie* is the source of a good deal of society's problems. It was this class that got rid of Louis XVI in the name of freedom and then proceeded to put the common man in chains. Of course, the contemporary *bourgeois* feels impelled to express his concern about the living conditions of the working class, but that, says Céline, is only "accident insurance," implying that if a revolution ever takes place the *bourgeoisie* might assure their survival by displaying in advance this kind of sympathy for workers. He adds, however — and we mention this because it is one of only two times that Jews are mentioned in this pamphlet — that if the *bourgeois*, in addition to displaying sympathy for the worker, also "smells a little Jewish," then this is all to his benefit too, for it is a kind of "life insurance." [6] What exactly did Céline mean by this? It is difficult to say for sure, but, given the idea that must have been already germinating in his mind and which would shortly come to full flower in *Bagatelles* and *Ecole*, France was seen as a country essentially owned and operated by Jews in which the native or Gentile population could exist only with the indulgence of their Jewish rulers. In this sense, then, smelling a bit Jewish is akin to assuring one's survival in a land run by Jews.

Perhaps the most concise way to bestow order on the arguments put forth by Céline in this work would be to describe his opposition to Communism in the following ways: (1) he hates the categorical and uncompromising materialism of Communism; (2) he despises its pretentions and the arrogance of its spokesmen in Russia, France, and elsewhere in the world; and (3) he detests its hypocrisy, its ultimate enshrinement of the lie as its main instrument of policy. With regard to the materialism of Communism, Céline rejects Engels' proposition that man is essentially what he eats. Filling man's belly and making him fat will not cure any of his problems, says Céline, for the evil in man is much too deeply engrained. Arguing like the Jansenist that he often seems to be in his writings, Céline points out that man is his own worst tyrant, and that dif-

ferences between workers and capitalists are artificial (as anybody
would see if true Socialism were imposed in the world by abolishing
inheritances). Without money and inheritances we would see what
human nature is really like, for then the wealthy exploiter would be
seen as no better or worse a person than the worker. The only thing
good about the church, he goes on, is that it has always told man
how terrible he is, how rotten, and what a stinking wretch he is,
how essentially evil and selfish his nature is.

In this context, that is, given the essential ugliness of man's
nature, Communism is no more than a plot, a huge hoax per-
petrated on the common man by a new class of rulers intent on
exploiting others and on maintaining their own privileges. In
Russia, the equivalent of the exploitative *bourgeoisie* is the party. It
controls everything, and its members are succeeded after their
death by their children. Their salaries and privileges are far out of
proportion to those of the rest of the nation, which they hold in
bondage by devoting most of the annual budget to the police,
propaganda, and the army. The only bright spot that Céline sees in
this materialistic, arrogant, lying dominance of a whole culture is
that man is basically like a rat. No matter how much you try to trap
him, he will sneak out of the snare just when you think you have
got him for good. In other words, the only thing that Céline is
hopeful and positive about in the Russian system is that, as
inhuman and devious as the system is, it still has met its match:
human selfishness will battle against it as much as possible.

The arrogance and self-satisfaction of the Soviet leaders piqued
Céline as much as did their materialism. "The people is king in
Russia," a slogan often offered by apologists of that country's
regime in the thirties, is twisted by Céline to the following: "In
Russia the people is King; he has everything but a shirt on his
back."[7]

In rebutting their claim to making man happier under the new
system than he had been under the old, Céline tells us that people
are so poor and deprived there that they try to buy the clothing off
the backs of Western visitors in the streets of Moscow. In fact, they
are so deprived and so miserable, he says, that the only thing they
are allowed to own is the future. Through propaganda about the
sharing of troubles and the longing look toward a luminous future,
the arrogant, self-righteous leaders of the ongoing Russian
Revolution coat the pill they are giving their people. Their

arrogance inevitably leads in Céline's mind to hypocrisy. Only a hypocrite, an inveterate liar, could call black white, poverty wealth, human misery and exploitation happiness and personal fulfillment. And yet they do this in Russia and get away with it before the eyes of the whole world. And one can't even complain over there, says Céline. At least in France you can bellow all you want, not that it will do you much good, but at least you can use your lung power to complain. No such avenue of protest is open in Russia, however. There, he says, everybody must dance, even the crippled. No one can sit on the sidelines there — you are either happy and dance along with the tune or there is no place for you.

In concluding, Céline sees the need to judge every revolution by what it leads to twenty years later. In this respect the Russian Revolution is a miserable failure. Despite the Soviets' arrogance and deviousness ("they have the nerve to try to dress up a turd, to pass it off as caramel!"[8]), the system is inhuman. Its essence is to destroy all those who do not agree with it and that, in the end, is the greatest indictment to be made against it. Céline, an outsider almost by nature, could well imagine the kind of life he would have had if he had been born in that unhappy land. At the very end of the pamphlet he refers again to Jews, this time as innocuously as he had earlier, stating that the system is rotten, and that "with Jews, without Jews all that is really of no importance."[9] Jews are irrelevant to the main argument of *Mea Culpa*, they figure only indirectly in the question. What is significant in this regard, however, is that within a short time after the publication of this work, the three main traits of the Communists that Céline denounces (materialism, arrogance, hypocrisy) will all be attributed to Jews, to all Jews, and have added to them a few half-baked racial theories borrowed from anti-Semitic texts he had read. For the common Russian man, whom he calls "Prolovitch" in *Mea Culpa*, and whom he sees as exploited by his leaders, he will substitute in the pamphlets the average Frenchman, whom he calls an "Aryan," and whom he considers to be exploited by Jews.

II   Bagatelles pour un massacre (Trifles for a Massacre)

Perhaps nowhere is criticism of Céline's work weakest, especially in the United States, than when it comes to objectively evaluating the pamphlets and their author. To begin with, these works have never been reprinted since the war, [10] let alone translated, so that one must make a special effort to get one's hands on the texts themselves. This being the case, some fairly influential critics seem to have foregone this difficulty of gaining access to the works and have simply presumed, from the titles of the works, that they called for the carrying out of Hitler's racial plans even before he had himself embarked on that gruesome course. As we shall see, this is very much like Joe McCarthy's accusing people in the midfifties of being responsible for the postwar partition of Europe and the subsequent cold war simply because they had been Communists or fellow travellers during the thirties.

Perhaps the best example of a critic losing touch with reality in order to smear Céline for something he neither did nor wrote is George Steiner's claim that Céline was guilty in his pamphlets of "famous and reiterated calls to mass murder," [11] and that his *Bagatelles* advocated "eradication of all Jews from Europe."[12] We have taken the trouble to read the pamphlets, as stated earlier, and nowhere in the text of these works are any such calls for mass murder made. But perhaps Steiner's distortions are as extreme as they are because he does not seem to have been able to understand how any Jewish critic (in this case, E. Ostrowsky) could find any redeeming value at all in Céline. Our task here, however, is not to quarrel with Steiner or with anyone else. We mention him only to remind the reader that we are quite aware that the subject at hand is a highly emotional one that rarely, if ever, has been treated calmly and rationally. This being said, we shall now try to describe as concretely and concisely as possible the content of the three hateful books that followed *Mea Culpa*.

The massacre that Céline had in mind when he entitled his first overtly anti-Semitic pamphlet *Bagatelles pour un massacre* was that of the "goïms," or Gentiles, whom he thought would be led to slaughter once again in another great war. Being convinced that World War I had been instigated by Jews in order to destroy the *aryen* races, he saw another war as inevitable. Throughout this work and in the next two pamphlets, he never at any time calls for annihilation of the Jews or for their extermination in the sense that the Nazis would later attempt to carry it out. On the contrary, the massacre mentioned in this work and the "cadavers" referred to in the title of *Ecole des cadavres* indicate only the rotting remains of Gentile victims of the next war since he presumes that in the next war, just as in the previous one, Jews will do their utmost to avoid military duty.

It is not insignificant that Céline dedicated this book to Eugène Dabit who had died only a year before while visiting the Soviet Union with Gide's group of anti-Fascist writers. Although Dabit, as a Communist sympathizer but not a member of the Communist Party, belonged to a group that was ideologically alien to the ties that Céline was in the process of creating for himself, Céline's dedication of the book to Dabit is patently transparent: he saw Dabit as a good example of the average French *aryen* of the midthirties. Poorly educated, from a humble economic background, Dabit had suffered a great deal while serving in the artillery during the first war and was haunted, as were many left wing writers like him, by the seeming inevitability of another war. Thus, in dedicating this book to Dabit, Céline was calling attention to the fact that if nothing else, he and Dabit were both "native" Frenchmen with roots going deep down into Gallic soil. They both suffered much during World War I, and if Dabit were still alive the politicians would be getting him ready for the next war. It should also be recalled that at the time of publication of the book Gide had finally gotten up the courage to denounce the Soviet system and was even going so far as to allege that the Soviets had killed Dabit, or at the very least refused to treat him when he fell ill because he had not been able to keep his mouth closed while in Russia. In a word, this dedication of the book to Dabit establishes an immediate connection with the previous pamphlet that denounced the Soviet Union but had nothing terribly potent or even offensive to say about Jews.[13]

Like *Mea Culpa*, this work rambles on and winds around itself, spilling forth hatred, venom, lies, and distortions as it goes. The link with *Mea Culpa* is most obvious in that Céline still talks in *Bagatelles* about the trip to Russia, condemning in more detail that country's health care delivery system as a sham and expressing his revulsion at the fact that someone had referred to him and Gide in the same breath, stating that they were both "renegades" who, although idolized by certain left wing critics, had still dared to criticize the Soviet Union. Enraged and insulted, Céline points out that he is quite different from Gide in that he did his criticizing while he was in Russia, whereas Gide waited until he was safely home before he dared express his disillusion. Underlining his

political independence and formally breaking with whatever
association he had ever had with the left because of his first two
novels, he states: "I adhere only to myself, as much as I can."[14] He
then claims that in this he is only an ordinary man: "Me, I've still
got the mind of a manual worker from before the war,"[15] that is,
simple, gullible, generous, exploited, desirous of improving his
economic lot, and possessor of racial hatreds and resentments that
need not be expressed for us to know that they are there.

And then the torrent begins. Taking up where *Mea Culpa* had
left off, *Bagatelles* sees the Jews as the inventors and propagators
of Communism: the movement is international in scope and will
eventually engulf all Frenchmen if they are not put on their guard.
Even overtly citing the discredited *Protocols of the Elders of Zion*
in the text (p. 279), he alleges that the leaders of the international
Jewish conspiracy have decided that war is the most effective and
efficient way of subverting the countries in which they live and that
this is why Jews all over the world, but especially in France,
England, and the United States, are howling for a declaration of
war against Germany. The judgments made about Communists in
Mea Culpa are now made about Jews, too: they are materialistic,
arrogant, and hypocritical, but that should not surprise anyone for
the words Jew and Communist mean the same thing, says Céline.

In the context of French life, Céline's vituperation is as strong as
anything ever written about Jews during the thirties or perhaps at
any other time in French history. He sees the masonic lodges as a
particularly strong haven of Jewish power and influence in
government. The university system has also been taken over by
Jews, as have all the arts. He knows this personally, he claims,
because a ballet that he wrote and had hoped to see performed was
rejected by the Jew (Jean Zay) who had the power to accept or
reject it.[16] All the professions have been taken over for that matter,
especially the one he knows from first hand experience, medicine.
There, Léon Blum has begun to allocate government posts
primarily to Jews (Céline, always the outsider, never had a formal
government appointment, with all the benefits that implies, while
he worked in clinics during the thirties), and it is they who get the
paid vacations, the top pay and perquisites,and the fat checks on
retirement.

The two main bastions of Jewish power are the USA and Russia.
"Hollywood la juive" and "Moscou la youtre"[17] are polluting

French life, the former with its outrageously Jewish-American movies, the latter with the fidelity with which French Jews defend its materialism and lying hypocrisy. Modern man, thanks to the influence of these two Jewish cultures, has been turned into a robot, so brutalized by machine work in the factory that his idea of genuine entertainment is to see Jewish movies sent from America. Unfortunately, the "indigenous" population of France is taken in by this. Pretty French girls are forever marrying Jews who seduce them with their wealth, and even something like the Nobel Prize is for sale, since everyone knows that Roger Martin du Gard received his prize for literature only because he had said a few flattering things about Jews and Dreyfus in one of his books!

But beyond all this claptrap, the idea of the inevitability of another war breaks through again and again. To Céline's mind — and he was not alone here, this conflict would probably take place on three fronts, with France (taking orders from England, the USA, and Moscow) obliged to bear the brunt of it all against Germany, Spain, and Italy. But this next war would be worse than the last one not only because it would most likely be waged on three fronts but also because it would use machines of destruction that were still undreamed of in 1918. Figures like five, ten, or 20 million deaths, chillingly correct, recur frequently in *Bagatelles*, and the only way to avoid this war, he argues, is to turn a deaf ear to the Jews who are screaming for a French war with Germany.

The volume ends after 379 pages, concluding with what he offers as the scenario for a "ballet." Just as he had begun the work with two ballets entitled, *Naissance d'une fée* (*Birth of a Fairy*) and *Voyou Paul brave Virginie* (*Loafer Paul Nice Virginia*), now he ends with one he calls *Van Bagaden*, a "grand ballet mime et quelques paroles" (p. 375). Critics have never really understood what the meaning of these ballets is in the context of the work, but Albert Chesneau has offered an explanation that is quite coherent and that goes far toward illuminating why Céline chose to place these "works" so strategically at the beginning and end of his pamphlet.[18] In a word, each of them depicts a conflict between an indigenous population and Outsiders or Invaders. He concludes convincingly: "The *ballets* are therefore not only poetic fantasies but also very transparent and very serious allegories that call for a return to basic sources, demand the expulsion of racially impure outsiders and preach a new crusade against them."[19] In all fairness to Céline though, it is one thing to expel or limit the power of Jews, and quite another thing to exterminate them.

III   Ecole des cadavres (School for Cadavers)

French Fascists and Anti-Semites who had applauded *Bagatelles* were floored by the appearance of *Ecole des cadavres* in 1938. In their view it could not have come out at a more inopportune time since Hitler had just won his greatest diplomatic triumph at Munich.[20] Nonetheless, Céline's *Ecole* applauds Hitler's politics and considers support for him necessary if Europe is to have peace. In fact, he is so strongly behind the Fascist regimes that he can write: "Personally, I find Hitler, Franco, Mussolini fabulously debonair, admirably magnanimous, infinitely too much after my own mind, in a word, bellowing pacifists worth 250 Nobel Prizes, hands down, by acclamation!"[21] Strangely enough, this is not the only place in *Ecole* where he mentions the Nobel Prize. He also does so at several other points in the book, leading this reader to believe with Chesneau that in his demented state he really believed that in backing the Fascist régimes he was truly serving the cause of peace. There are several other important citations in *Ecole* that were not made in *Bagatelles* and in which Céline indicates the sources of some of his ideas: "Every Aryan should have read Drumont. More up to date: De Vries, De Poncins, Sombart, Stanley Chamberlain, still closer: Montandon, Darquier de Pellepoix, Boissel, H.-R. Petit, Dasté, H. Coston, Des Essards, Alex, Santo, etc. ... You'll find a very widely used French bibliography at the *Centre Documentaire*, 10 rue d'Argenteuil, au Rassemblement anti-juif, 12 rue Laugier."[22]

But if Céline followed the German line in foreign policy and accepted the anti-Semitic views of the above-mentioned fanatics, does this mean that he advocated, to repeat Steiner's phrase, the "eradication of all Jews from the face of Europe?" No. In fact, it is in *Ecole* that he offers his own view of what Frenchmen should do in reaction to what he considered to be the Jewish domination of French life: "If Daladier really wanted to even things up, as he said, he didn't have to pass 500 laws. Three good, effective ones would take care of it: (1) Expulsion of all Jews, (2) Outlawing and closing of all Masonic Lodges and secret societies, (3) Hard labor for life for all who are dissatisfied, hard of hearing, etc. ..."[23]

Where would the Jews go once they left France? To England, the United States, Russia, and Palestine, countries they control already, says Céline. But they would not be exterminated.

There are several other themes that Céline reiterates in this book and that are worth mentioning here. The first is that until the year 843 when the Treaty of Verdun split what had been Charlemagne's empire into three distinct branches that have evolved into modern day Italy, Germany, and France, Aryans in Northern Europe solidly supported each other and lived in harmony.[24] Since that time, the Aryans have been split among themselves into warring camps so that the destructive work of Jews has been that much easier for them to accomplish. And since international Jewry is really the world's only international movement, they have been quite well situated for carrying out their designs. Another point about this book that is made more blatantly than in the earlier *Bagatelles* is that Céline overtly praises the virtues of that class for which *Bagatelles* had been written: the *petite bourgeoisie*. To him (pp. 142 - 150 for example) this is France's most industrious class, having none of the self-destructive traits of the working class (sloth, stupidity, and alcoholism among others) but yet not reaping the rewards that their work ought to garner for them since they are outmaneuvered from above by the privileged classes, notably the upper *bourgeoisie* rotten with Jews.

To make matters worse, says Céline, it is always this class that is decimated in wartime. It is this group, therefore — the small shopkeeper-artisans and other small-time functionaries and self-employed people — who should reject the Jewish plot to start another war.

One last point is also made strongly in this book, namely that England, corrupted and directed by Jews, will be only too eager to see the two Aryan groups (French and German) that lived in harmony prior to 843 go to war against each other once more. British intelligence, he claims, is a direct arm of the international Jewish conspiracy and the only way for Frenchmen to block their plan is to rally behind a Franco-German alliance that would bring together once and for all two peoples that racially are really only one.[25]

It is on this call for a political and military alliance as the best assurance of peace that Céline ends the book, and in a sense everything he states therein can be understood in terms of this political vision. Thus, the Pope is a Jew! And of course the twelve apostles were all Jews too! For in preaching an effeminate religion that eventually stripped the naturally alert and warlike Aryan of his manly qualities and made him a servant of Jews, they have contributed to the rule of France by Jews and her division from Germany.[26] Similarly, Maurras, that fervent, devoted, and unmitigated anti-Semite, is also dismissed as a "Jew," as are contemporary Fascists like La Rocque and Doriot, presumably because they did not share Céline's fervor for a Franco-German alliance. Finally, a few further points ought to be made about *Bagatelles* and *Ecole*. As Pol Vandromme,[27] who considers Céline to be a child, a *grand naïf* in politics, has pointed out, people usually consider these two pamphlets as the product of a cynical mind. But when one stops to realize that the same man who took five years to write *Voyage* and another four years to write *Mort* wrote both *Bagatelles* and *Ecole* in a short space of several months, one begins to comprehend that Céline, who interrupted other work in process, quite possibly really believed that he could change his countrymen's minds by writing these pamphlets. But instead of treating his subject in the form of a philosophical pamphlet designed to argue his viewpoint rationally against adversaries, he used every rhetorical trick in his arsenal to put his point across. It is as if, like the prophet Ezekiel, to whom he is often ironically compared by Vandromme, he hoped to sway people, to change their minds and make them see what he took to be the truth by scolding them.[28]

IV   Les Beaux draps (A Nice Mess)

When *Les Beaux draps* appeared in 1941, Paris was already occupied by the *Wehrmacht* and Céline himself had already returned to the capital after having first attempted to serve in the French Army against Germany. Refused for medical reasons, he then proceeded to do all he could as a volunteer in the medical service during the summer of 1940 as the *Wehrmacht* pursued what was left of the French Army, as well as hundreds of thousands of fleeing French civilians, from the Rhine to the Atlantic.

In this his last pamphlet, Céline goes beyond the social doctrine expounded in *Ecole*. Here, instead of extolling the virtues of the class he considered to be his own, the *petite bourgeoisie*, he attacks the class he holds responsible for all of France's troubles, the *haute bourgeoisie.* It is this class, he claims, full of Jews, of course, but in which many Gentiles play along with the Jews to maintain their privileges, that has brought about the debacle. The religion of this class is materialism and what has made matters worse is that, since the Jewish-led Popular Front of 1936, this class has not only gotten richer (thanks to the series of devaluations the Popular Front government was forced to enact), but it has also infected the working class to a degree unknown before. Rejecting the common working man as the "suckling little brother of the Bourgeois"[29] at the beginning of the book, Céline then sets about trying to destroy any other illusions his reader might entertain.

For Céline, nobody wants to sacrifice anything anymore in this age of rampant materialism.[30] Democracy is an upper *bourgeois* tool designed to keep the working man in his place. For if the classes in power were really serious about dealing with France's social injustices and inequalities, they would create a system in which everyone would be paid the same salary (he suggests 150 francs a month for everyone). In this way the class system would disappear and a real system of National Socialism, Céline style, would come into being.

But it is probably impossible to install such a politicoeconomic system, he states, since the common Frenchman is so asinine that he really does not even care any more about being exploited. His mind is so rotted by watching movies that he, like the *bourgeois* who is typically consumed by avarice, can be said to be consumed by his own vice, *ennui* (boredom). Michelet and Gobineau, he declares, were crazy to try to sing the praises of the Gallic race, for the French are only a gang of jokers who do not deserve any praise (pp. 124 - 126). In fact they are so stupid and so easily led that the same people who hated the English only months before for not coming to help them against the German *Blitzkrieg* and for running out on them at Dunkirk instead of sharing the disaster with the French, are now sanctimoniously putting their faith in De Gaulle and his friends in England. But money and manipulation can achieve amazing results, he adds.

Some of the previous themes do recur once again in this book, though. More than ever conscious of being an outsider, someone who is persecuted irrationally by forces of evil (Jews), he claims that he is free of all the common vices that cripple his countrymen. Having always practiced medicine among the poor for little or no pay, and never having made a political statement for his own benefit, he implies that he is somehow better situated than others to make the judgments contained in his book. His famous statement to the effect that "I didn't wait for the German High Command to be set up at the Hotel Crillon before becoming pro-German,"[31] is indicative of the somewhat sanctimonious, I-told-you-so tone of the book. Of course, at the time this book first appeared, in May of 1941, American intervention in the war was only a short way off and German troops were about to undergo their first serious reversals in Russia.

Nonetheless, if we examine the phrase closely, we see that here, as elsewhere in this book, he is beginning to express his disappointment in Hitler and in his army for not bringing a true revolution to France. Ridiculing the collaborators who decided to go along with the Germans only at the last minute and who therefore do not even know how to spell such a common German word (in occupied France) as *Kommandatur* (headquarters), he also mocks the Germans for strutting like peacocks through the most exclusive places in Paris. For the fact of the matter is that Céline seems to have naively written his pamphlets and supported Hitler because he really believed that a true revolution that would abolish class distinctions was a genuine possibility if Hitler were to be able to exert some influence on the French political scene. This fact is born out by the curious interview that took place between Céline and Lucien Rebatet, co-editor of the Fascist weekly *Je Suis Partout*. Rebatet recalls visiting Céline during the month of October 1940, at a time when German fortunes in the war were perhaps at their height. He remembers the date especially because Céline told him at the time that he was sure the Germans would lose the war — and that in fact they had no chance at all of winning. When asked why he thought this way, he replied: "They're finished, and us too. An army that doesn't bring a revolution along with it in a war like this is cooked. The Krauts are finished."[32] Thus the visionary crying out for a complete social revolution in which French society would be rebuilt from the bottom up would not see that revolution take place in his day, although the events of 1968 and the issues that came to the fore during the presidential campaign of 1974 called attention to many of the kinds of social changes Céline wanted to see take place.

The hatred of Communism as an international Jewish plot is

quite visible in the pages of this book for it represents above all else to Céline the triumph of unmitigated materialism. He claims that New York Jews like Loeb and Warburg (pp. 98 - 111) actually financed the Russian Revolution and concludes that Jews are so deeply involved with this monster they have created with the intention of taking over the world that the monster itself is the only thing that inspires fear in them. To him the Jew "is afraid of only one thing: Communism without Jews." [33]

But although Jews are hated and vilified in this book as much as in the earlier ones, his main quarrel here seems to be with the injustice of France's social system. He does not call for the expulsion of Jews in this book, and at times attacks professional anti-Semites for using the issue to their own benefit. For example, in attacking the anti-Semitic press that flourished during the Vichy regime, he exclaims: "It makes you sick, all the supposedly wildly anti-Semitic newspapers, what do they really want? You wonder. What do they want? To take the place of the Yids? Put themselves in their places? That's a very skimpy program." [34] In other words, even the collaborators are as rotten with materialism as those who usually receive Céline's scorn, for they serve to perpetuate the cleavage in the social system whereby the mass of the population is kept relatively poor, divided, and exploited while the elite enjoys its privileges. Then, regarding the privileged classes, he bellows "The elite is example or it's nothing" [35] toward the end of the book. And in those dark days during 1941, while the shadow of occupation and collaboration lay across the breadth of France, Céline for one was sure that the only example the elite gave was one of hypocrisy, arrogance, and materialism, vices he had earlier associated first with Communists, then with Jews, and now too with the elite, the ruling *haute bourgeoise* class in French society.

In conclusion, it seems to us that to claim, as some critics like Poulet and Vandromme, have done, that Céline was really not an anti-Semite but only used the motif of *juif* as a kind of symbol, a code word that really meant exploiter or hypocrite, is to hide one's head in the sand. Reading the pamphlets at a distance of almost forty years cannot change the fact that although there is at times the use of the word *juif* as a symbol of the fat cat who gets wealthy exploiting the labor of others, of manipulating politicians and lying to gain his own ends, one cannot help but conclude that, at this time of Céline's life anyway, he had a violent hatred of Jews as people. In addition to this first, somewhat evasive, response to the problem, a second explanation of Céline's attitude toward Jews argues that his anti-Semitism was a passing phenomenon that did not appear earlier and was also not visible in his later works. According to this view, expounded for example by Albert Chesneau, Céline seems to have gone through a crisis that led him to see the Jew not only as a symbol but as a *cause* of all evil.[16] The crisis came at a bad time in history and almost cost Céline his life, but it was no more, according to this view, than a passing crisis.

This explanation follows the road of "psychocriticism," and concludes that, although Céline was not terribly fond of Jews at this particular period of his life, the fact that Jews are generally absent from his work both before and after the era of the pamphlets indicates that the word Jew did indeed have for him a special symbolic value at the time he was one of France's most ardent anti-Semites. According to this view, and we are following Chesneau here, Céline's problems began as a child who viewed himself as a grotesque creature surrounded by grotesque parents. By extention, Jews become symbols of the "parents grotesques" syndrome, and in order to free himself from the threat they posed to him psychologically he had to create another image of himself and of the land in which he lived by returning to the past to an age when such ugliness had not yet come into existence. Interestingly, and this is a provocative if somewhat gratituous point of view, Chesneau concludes that Céline never should have written *Mort à crédit*, for that novel reawakened in him hatreds for his parents and his early childhood that had been brought under control until that time. Once set free by the writing of the book, though, they would lead by extension to his period of anti-Semitism.

A third explanation places the emphasis on events in Céline's life that seem to have taken place around the time he was getting ready to write the pamphlets and which might indeed have provoked him to write them in the first place. These events are not necessarily limited to the following, but we at least know that the following events did take place: his ballet that was turned down and therefore never produced — an event he complains about loudly in *Bagatelles* — is generally said to have been sabotaged by a Jew, in this case, Jean Zay, who was minister of information at the time. Elizabeth Craig, an American dancer with whom he lived for a while in Paris and to whom he dedicated *Voyage*, left Céline to marry an

American lawyer who was also Jewish. Céline is also said to have been ejected from his position at the Clichy clinic, where he had already worked for years, because he did not get along with an East European Jew who was appointed over his head and who therefore had the power to fire him. Finally, it is said that Céline was particularly annoyed at the Popular Front government because Léon Blum, against the advice of the Grand Rabbi of Strasburg, went ahead and showed preference to Jews in allocating positions in his government. All these events, occurring during the thirties between the time of composition of *Voyage* and the publication of *Bagatelles*, are said to have been contributing factors to Céline's dislike for the Jewish presence in his and in France's life.[37]

A fourth possible explanation for Céline's conduct at the time of writing the pamphlets is that he was slightly out of his mind if not downright crazy.[38] But we reject this somewhat simple assessment just as we reject categorically Gide's contention that Céline was only exaggerating when he wrote *Bagatelles*. Likewise, Sartre also completely misses the mark when he writes in, "Portrait de l'antisémite," that "If Céline could support the social theses of the Nazis, it is because he was paid to do so."[39] Sartre, whose first novel, *La Nausée* (1938), owes much to Céline, was disappointed in Céline's later politics, but he never denied the effect that *Voyage* had had on him.

A fifth and last explanation of the problem is outlined by Patrick McCarthy in his biography of Céline. Following Sartre's lead in defining the anti-Semite as someone who in reality hates himself and who, in abandoning his reason in order to hate Jews, is ultimately fleeing from an awareness of himself, McCarthy then pushes this view one step further than Sartre by pointing out that Céline had a special antipathy for Jews because, as a hated people and as symbols of the persecuted and martyred of the earth, they competed directly with the image that he wanted to project of himself as an outcast and a pariah. In stifling them, he defined and reaffirmed his own importance.[40] We find this argument a weighty one, especially when coupled with the fact that Céline had pointed out in writing *Voyage* that he was involved in a life or death struggle with his own innate pessimism about the human condition. By the time he had written *Mort à crédit*, travelled to Russia, and returned to write *Mea Culpa*, the pessimism of Robinson had won out over Bardamu's openness to life.

In addition to all these explanations of the problem of Céline's anti-Semitism, we should also recall that Céline was an adamant antimilitarist and pacifist. His *Voyage*, one of the greatest antiwar novels of all time, proves this point. Thus, he wrote, at least in part, in the hope that his countrymen would not rush headlong into another senseless war. Céline's social class has also been one that has historically been one in which anti-Semitism has flourished. Growing up at a time when the Dreyfus affair was dividing France against herself, he in all probability heard of the affair as a child mainly from the antidreyfusard point of view. He then spent his childhood in the back room of his mother's shop — a kind of business that was slowly being driven out of competition by the rise of large scale department stores which the French lower *bourgeois* often associated with Jews. As stated above, he makes much of belonging to this class in *Ecole*, reminding his readers that they will be the ones to die if the Jews have their way and start another war. Furthermore, there is reason to believe that Céline never felt himself at home among intellectuals even after he became a literary celebrity with *Voyage*. At this time more than ever he seems to have affected the manners and comportments of the petty Parisian, as if to underline to the intellectuals on the left bank that he was really not one of them.

We should also recall that the small private-owned business, characterized ideally by the accumulation of a small fortune through a lifetime of work, and the notion of private property were also ingrained in Céline. His trip to Russia and the vision he had there of a kind of life that would have extinguished for good the impulse for economic independence so typical of the petty *bourgeois* Frenchman led him to completely reject the Soviet model. And as pointed out earlier, it did not take long for the recriminations heaped on the heads of Communists (for their materialism, arrogance, and hypocrisy) in *Mea Culpa* to be attributed to Jews in *Bagatelles*. Hating Communism and war, both of which he associated with Jews, he wanted to avoid another blood bath and the only way he thought this was possible would be to write the pamphlets. Apparently composing hundreds of pages and then cutting them down to form what are still rather stout volumes, he rushed to complete his books before the war came.

Finally, Céline remained a racially conscious person until the day he died. Even someone like the present writer, who admires only his

Voyage as a truly essential book, must recognize that fact. He states at the end of *Rigodon*, for example, which he completed only hours before he died: "It's only the blood that counts." [41] Earlier in the same book he laments that "Europe died at Stalingrad," [42] and, calling himself a "biologist," decrees that "only biology matters" and that "yellow and black always win over white." [43] For someone who has closely read the pamphlets, it is obvious that Céline had not really changed by the end of his life, but had merely learned to present his thought in a more acceptable manner. In these later books he talks about the Chinese taking over the West, using "Chinese" in the same way that "Jew" had been used earlier, but the same obsession with outsiders and with non-Aryans is still all too obvious. And just because the code word "Jew" was dropped in later years, this does not make his essentially anti-Semitic pamphlets any less odious.

In this context, then, of the social class background, the ardent unflinching pacifism, the naiveté of the middle-aged moralist who was nearing forty when he became a literary celebrity, and the latent racism that came to the fore in the middle thirties when anti-Semitism was in certain ways fashionable, we can begin to understand what prompted Céline to write his pamphlets. When we add to these complex factors the possibility that Céline might have also been impotent, that he was essentially a pessimist who enjoyed being an outsider, and that he had a series of unfortunate run-ins with people who just happened to be Jewish, the composition of the pamphlets becomes less of a surprise and more comprehensible — although no less excusable — in the total context of his life.

Finally, when we state that Céline was a racist until the end of his life, we do not mean that he did not recognize that he had over-stated his case in the pamphlets. The conclusion that he remained forever a racially conscious person is inescapable from a reading of his later work, but, although he retained this biological con-sciousness until the end, this does not mean that he was proud of what he had written in the pamphlets. The best proof of this is that he apparently asked his wife to see to it that they would never be republished again. Thus *Bagatelles*, *Ecole*, and *Beaux Draps* remain very difficult to get hold of — and this is as it should be. They represent a sure turn for the worse on the part of a great writer. After having written them, as if cursed for having misused his lyrical gifts, Céline would never again regain the verbal power displayed in *Voyage* and *Mort*.

CHAPTER 5

The Return to French Letters

I   Guignol's Band I *and* II

G uignol's Band was most likely written during the war years
while Céline was residing in Paris. As we know, he took flight
from France a short time after the Allied landings in June 1944,
and *Guignol's Band* was published just before he left for Germany.
In the opening pages of this four hundred page volume he announced that only the first part was being published for the time
being and alluded to a complete text of some twelve hundred
(presumably manuscript) pages. Thus, *Guignol's Band* was from
the very beginning a truncated work for which, it was thought, a
sequel or completion would be forever lost. In fact, it was only in
1962, a year after Céline's death, that his secretary accidentally
stumbled upon the rest of the manuscript whose continued
existence Céline himself probably had already despaired of.
Published under the title *Pont de Londres* (*London Bridge*),[1] a title
suggested by the *céliniste* Robert Poulet, this second volume is a
five hundred page work which, although it brings its narration to
completion, does not seem to have been completely corrected by
Céline. For all practical purposes, however, *Guignol's Band II* can
be considered as a completed novel which, like *Guignol's Band I*,
was probably written before Céline's departure from Paris in the
summer of 1944.

The novel begins with a five page statement of aesthetic conviction on the part of the older narrator who speaks using the first
person "je" and who is presumably the same older narrator who
had begun *Mort* and then relinquished the narrative function to the
younger Ferdinand. Here he claims that his editor did not like
Guignol's Band when he first read it, finding it coarse, crude,
vulgar, and boring, and nothing but a long, tedious, seemingly
unending tale dealing only with a series of brawls. But then, claims

118

Céline, after it was realized what he was trying to do, the book was accepted. Apparently most resistance centered not on the subject matter of the novel, but on the way Céline told his story, using the three dots instead of writing conventional prose sentences. Books written in such a way, he had to confess, seemed to him "sketchy, unwritten, stillborn, neither finished nor likely to be, lifeless." [2] Claiming still to possess all of the florid pages his grandfather Auguste, the former *lycée* teacher at Le Havre, had written, he categorically and voluntarily rejects all use of traditional rhetoric. The style he is aiming to create is one that reflects his own temperament and is also, he feels, in keeping with the tempo of his century: "Jazz knocked out the waltz, impressionism killed 'faux-jour,' you'll write in 'telegraphic' or you won't write at all." [3] Of course, these few words deal with the *forme* of his novels. As usual he has nothing to say about their *fond*, but he does seem sure that in two hundred years his books will be read by French school children the way the classics are today. [4]

After this apologia for his style of writing, the older narrator suddenly jumps to a different subject for the next twenty-five pages or so, describing in vivid detail an imagined air attack on Orleans and then rambling on about his relationship to his critics, readers, and fellow citizens. These pages are nothing more than disorganized dribble that seem to have been written after the first part of the novel itself, which might have been begun before 1940. They also reflect the confused ravings of a besieged mind that is still lucid enough to know that people can despise him for reasons other than the fact that he uses four letter words in his books. But he seems to have preferred to believe that all hostility to him sprang from a lack of comprehension of his literary objectives. This smoke screen is even less convincing now than it was in 1944.

The word *guignol* in French usually refers to a kind of marionnette show, the "Grand Guignol," that inspires deep emotion in children because of the extremes of human behavior that it can depict. The word can also be used to refer figuratively to a human being who is comic and ridiculous, and once one begins reading this novel, one sees that it is this meaning that Céline ostensibly wants to give to the word. The older narrator, who is in fact none other than Céline himself, will gaze back in the course of the next nine hundred pages on the foolish and laughable youth that he once was and on the "band" of characters he came to know while residing in London during World War I. Transposing his memories of this period in his life, he will paint a picture of life that is more deliberately comical in intent than either *Voyage* or *Mort*. But at the same time the novel ultimately fails in large part because it lacks the snarling indignation and the discovery of a deep and painful existential hurt that had made *Voyage* such a great novel.

Guignol's Band I and *II* show the older narrator indulging in joyful and detailed descriptions of things and objects, like, for instance, the celebrated passage in which he describes his childlike enthusiasm for the excitement generated by the busy life along the Thames. Here, the river's warehouses, cranes, ships, and overall hustle and bustle fill him with a joy and wonder, and, it seems, an acceptance of modern mechanized society. And when he talks of London's dockside children as "laughing angels"[5] whom he will always fondly remember, one wonders if this novelist is the same man who had so strongly attacked England and the English in his pamphlets. Switching back and forth at times between the use of the older narrator who begins the story, and that of the younger Ferdinand who recounts the action as he lives it, Céline is able to poke fun at the comical and farcical creature that Ferdinand was in his youth. He just cannot take the boy seriously in this book.

After the rambling opening pages, the older narrator presents Borokrom, a piano player in various London pubs who seems to have been a bomb-throwing anarchist in days gone by. As is often the case among small-time underworld types, legend surrounds the truth of one's past and Céline seems to want us to share the wonderment of the world he is recreating and transposing for us by giving us only the amount of information we would have about these people if we were actually members of the band in London.

But now the youthful Ferdinand takes up the narrative and tells of his wanderings in wartime London where he has come after having been wounded in action. He is taken in by the pimp Cascade whose "band" of prostitutes will supply Céline with an unending sequence of comically grotesque situations and actions until the end of the novel. Since Ferdinand's papers are not in order — much like Robinson's in *Voyage* — Scotland Yard is on his tail. They also want to talk to him about his presence at a bombing — an act that his friend Borokrom committed to stop a pub brawl. Further wanderings take Ferdinand to the shop of an eccentric pawnbroker named Titus Van Claben who dresses in Oriental clothes and who

"says things to himself in a sort of Yiddish." [6] There he joins
Borokrom, who is already quite drunk, Van Claben, and the
latter's maid, Delphine. When Titus undergoes an asthma attack,
they send Delphine out for medicine but when she comes back it is
not with the remedy that Van Claben ordinarily takes but with
"eucalyptus" cigarettes that they all begin smoking. Soon drugged
and delirious, they begin an orgy with Van Claben and his maid
pairing off while Boro expresses his interest in Ferdinand. When
Van Claben, lying on his bed, gathers his money bags together and
spreads his wealth out before himself on his belly, the drugged trio
of Boro, Ferdinand, and Delphine proceed to stuff him with his
money. When Van Claben then lapses into unconsciousness, Boro
first squeezes his Adams' apple to get the money out of him and
relieve his indigestion. When that procedure does not work, he and
Ferdinand bounce the man on his head. But by now he is dead.

Not wanting to return to the band, Ferdinand takes flight but is
spotted and followed by the midget Mille-Pattes, an employee of
Cascade. While waiting for a subway train together, Ferdinand
nudges the midget under the oncoming cars. But this act will not
solve his problems either for Inspector Matthew from Scotland
Yard had been on the opposite platform all the time watching what
was going on. So Ferdinand flees once more, but now his
predicament is so bad that he goes to the French Consulate and
demands to be permitted to reenlist in the army, for service at the
front could not be more dangerous than life for him in London
where, he suspects, there must be some kind of a plot afoot to get
him into trouble. While at the consulate he meets Sosthène de
Rodiencourt, a would-be magus who claims that he would like to
go to Tibet in search of the "flower of the Magi" that would allow
him access to the fourth dimension. But like most con men, and
Sosthène should be taken as not much more than that, he will be
quite happy with a reasonable amount of financial security as long
as he, and his American wife, do not have to work. He takes
Ferdinand on as his assistant and then, somewhat like Don Quixote
and Sancho Panza who ride off on horseback in quest of adventure, these two heroes ride off, at the very end of *Guignol's
Band I*, on city bus number 29.

The object of their bus ride is to get in touch with the inventor of
of gas masks, one Colonel J. F. C. O'Colloghan, who is allegedly
preparing a test model of a gas mask which, he hopes, will even-

tually be put into production by the British government. But no
sooner does Ferdinand arrive at the colonel's house than he falls in
love with the man's niece, Virginia. A courtship reminiscent of the
title that Céline gave to his ballet *Voyou Paul brave Virginie*,
(*Loafer Paul Nice Virginia*) [7] follows in which the young narrator
seems to be constantly telling us of his desire to indulge in every
imaginable sexual act with the girl. His imagination is finally
gratified when, after having visited a nightclub with Virginia, they
copulate and then find their way back home to the colonel's house
(where Sosthène and Ferdinand share a room upstairs, for by this
time Sosthène's wife has gone off with a certain Nelson). Céline, in
these pages dealing with the youthful lust of an adolescent, plays
the copulation scene between Virginia and Ferdinand for maximum
effect. The same youth who, still unsure of himself, had fought off
Borokrom's homosexual advances earlier, now goes all out to
seduce Virginia who, physically worn out and presumably having
had a few drinks, succumbs.

Now a new situation obtains at the colonel's house. He forbids
his niece to have anything to do with Ferdinand, and in the
meantime Sosthéne is used as a comic vehicle, for he is more and
more afraid that the government might use real gas on the day of
the gas mask trials. He thus tries to get us to believe that a spirit
named Goa lives within him, going so far as to meditate on Goa's
presence in the midst of Piccadilly Circus, an act for which he is
roundly beaten by the police. But then, just before the day of the
trials, the colonel disappears and Inspector Matthew also comes
snooping around again. The trio of Virginia, Sosthène, and Ferdinand thus decide to take flight in the hope of leaving England
altogether. Ferdinand gets an underworld character named
Prospero Jim to put him in touch with someone who can smuggle
him out of the country to Latin America, and he even goes so far as
to tell his two companions that he is about to leave without them —
a decision about which neither is very happy — when Prospero tells
him that first he must have a drink because it is his patron saint's
day — Saint Ferdinand's Day. The drinking begins and before we
know it the whole band has been assembled again. Ferdinand, who
has been suffering from insomnia for some time now and suspects
that army surgeons had left a piece of steel in his head when they
operated on him, causing him to hear a constant buzzing in his
ears, now proceeds to describe for us the huge orgy that takes place

while the city is bombarded by German Zeppelins flying above. In the midst of the *fête*, Van Claben's cadaver, now four months old, is brought in by Boro and Doctor Clodo, and then it is disposed of in the river. Surprised and relieved, Ferdinand slips out of the party with Virginia and Sosthène, crosses London Bridge, and leaves the band behind.

Finally, at the very end of the novel we get the impression that he will also soon leave behind both Virginia and Sosthène, for, as they cross the bridge, these two physically exhausted and somewhat inebriated characters keep trying to get Ferdinand to make faces, to clown it up to amuse them, but he refuses. The Ferdinand whom we have already met in *Voyage* and *Mort*, the hero who would eventually come to terms and compromise with the demands of society, is here about to embark on those adventures that begin with the African adventure in *Voyage*. His foolish youthful days are behind him. There is no ultimate truth in drugs, alcohol, sex, or love. That Ferdinand whom Céline remembered fondly while writing *Guignol's Band* no longer exists at the end of the novel. Instead, he is at the threshold of becoming the lucid Bardamu who will look more and more deeply into himself as he advances in age and whose struggle to find himself will be chronicled in *Voyage*.

There is no way that we can separate the two parts of *Guignol's Band* from *Voyage* and *Mort* because, stylistically, they represent the full fruition of the so-called telegraphic style. But at the same time, they backtrack and complete our knowledge of Ferdinand's psychological journey from the passage des Bérésinas where he spent his earliest days in *Mort*, through the early war years that are only rapidly described in *Voyage*, to the final point where, at the end of the night, the rebellious side of Bardamu/Robinson must be disposed of in order for Ferdinand to go on accepting the absurdity of his existence.

As mentioned above, the "guignol" of the title refers specifically to the hero of the work who, first and foremost, is seen by Céline as a comic and ridiculous character. The stage of life through which this lower middle class everyman is passing is that of adolescence, the period of apprenticeship during which one traditionally sows one's wild oats. For this reason the recurrence of delirium scenes in which the younger narrator has less and less of a grasp on what is really happening around him, is pivotal to our comprehension of what Céline is trying to say in this work. Still uneducated, and condemned by circumstances to killing time in England while the rest of civilization goes about destroying itself in Europe, Ferdinand gradually learns that all existence is basically deceptive and confusing, and that reality is at best a nebulous concept. This understanding is most forcefully expressed in the sentence describing Ferdinand's disbelief at the wild happenings that surround him in the great orgy and air attack scene near the end of *Pont de Londres*, when he states that "I felt like a waking dreamer." [8] The very phrase *reveur éveillé* brings to mind the study by Léon Daudet entitled *Le Rêve éveillé*, a book that unfortunately has not received the critical attention it deserves and that might have first communicated to Céline this notion of a subconscious or at least subliminal state of consciousness that continues to function even during our waking hours and not just during our sleep. Céline of course has taken this idea — and we believe that in fact he did get it from Daudet — and built upon it his whole concept of delirium, a kind of state of mental breakdown into which the mind seems to lapse when reality becomes too overpowering or stressful.

Thus this youth who in the beginning of *Voyage* has learned of the insanity of war, a war defended and deeply desired by all the leaders of the civilizations of the rational West, now learns of the underside of reality, that side that is made up of people who are by preference out of stride with what society considers to be important. Consorting with prostitutes, pimps, freaks, a madman like O'Colloghan, and a con man like Sosthène, he thinks he has found some meaning in the midst of it all when he thinks he is in love with Virginia. But that sentiment too seems to pass, and by the end of the novel, as he crosses London Bridge, he is no longer willing to play a comic role, that is, to be a *guignol*, just to please her. The antiwar theme is also ever present here just as it had been in *Voyage*, for we are occasionally reminded that the reason for all this madness in the first place is that the war is going on. Céline also lashes out against social injustice in this novel, but the outcries are muted for the simple reason that Ferdinand is still too naive and too young to understand where he fits into the overall social panorama. Only later, after more travel and the acquisition of an education, will he fully understand the darkness of it all.

Finally, the ridiculous and comical character that is Ferdinand in *Guignol's Band I* and *II* is someone who, because of his essential foolishness, cannot help running into and bouncing off other comical types. Céline's target in this novel is laughter. He wants to laugh at his hero (at that stage of his life when the hero, thinking he knows everything about life, still really knows almost nothing) who proclaims in solemn tones his love for Virginia even though she becomes pregnant; who falls under the influence of a con man (who was probably slightly mad as well) like Sosthène; and who has himself conned into staying around for a party that turns into an orgy even though he has just resolutely decided and then announced to all that he is leaving to begin a new life in South America. The novel is replete with incidents like these in which Céline pokes fun at his hero. But there is also another laughter that Céline is aiming at in *Guignol* — the laughter that the reader enjoys in descriptions of scenes like the ones describing orgies; the murder of Van Claben, who seems to be killed almost inadvertantly; and the deflowering of Virginia by an overanxious Ferdinand, a scene which in this reader's mind is one of the most comical descriptions of sexual intercourse to be found in modern literature. The book seems to complete our knowledge of Ferdinand's journey while at the same time allowing Céline to push even further along in his development of the telegraphic style, exploring both its possibilities and limitations.

Ultimately, however, the reader is overwhelmed by it all, just as Céline hints that his editor was flabbergasted when he brought the manuscript in to him. The work is overly long and could have benefited from expurgation, just as his earlier books presumably did. The narrative line is basically so thin that it just cannot withstand nine hundred pages of dense prose. There are pages of power and insight in both of these volumes, and in fact there is Célinian writing of a power here that vies with his best work, but we see it only in patches. On the other hand, for someone who has read the first two novels, the atmosphere here is somewhat like that of a May day after lengthy days of April showers. It is nice to discover that the sun is still in the sky, and that all that bleakness and negativism do not represent the whole picture. But this is true only because the period of Ferdinand's life that is analyzed here is one that naturally lends itself to comedy. [9] The youth who will soon learn that life is not a joke will not, as an adult, be able to laugh or even smile at life. But Céline also seems to be saying that although we already know that person and the choices he has made (having read the earlier novels), one can still find some humor amidst the sadness of life, some brief glimpses of light in the darkness, and still clutch at a sentimental attachment or two while doggedly hanging on to one's lucidity.

II   Féerie pour une autre fois I *and* II
(Fairyland For Another Time)

The publication of *Féerie pour une autre fois* in 1952 [10] by Gallimard marked an important turning point in Céline's career, for if Gaston Gallimard had not bought the rights the previous year to *Voyage*, *Mort* and *Guignol's Band I*, and in so doing provided Céline with an income advance against future work, the remainder of Céline's career as a writer would most surely have developed differently. First of all, since he was penniless and still in exile in 1951, one wonders how Céline would have gone on living without his contract from Gallimard. But we must also remember that although this financial support enabled him to continue to live and work, it also called for publication of future manuscripts. These future works, especially the two volumes of *Féerie pour ue autre fois*, the second of which is called *Normance: Féerie pour une autre fois II* (1954), are by far the weakest and most repetitive books that Céline ever wrote. Disjointed and virtually plotless, and often used by the author to justify his past political conduct, they remind us of the most dismal aspects of the pamphlets, but at the same time they foreshadow the last three volumes, *D'un chateau l'autre*, *Nord*, and *Rigodon*, in which he will tell of his experiences in Germany and Denmark at the closing days of the war and after. Interestingly, in both volumes of *Féerie* he omits to mention, in the list of books previously written by him and which one usually finds inside the cover of most French books, his prior authorship of *Mea Culpa, Bagatelles pour un massacre, Ecole des cadavres,* or *Les Beaux draps*. He seems to want his reader to forget that he ever wrote a polemical word in his life, but then, once we start reading *Féerie I*, we find the author almost constantly reminding us of his past activities. Of course this seeming contradiction is resolved if it was Gallimard, as some critics now think, who deleted mention of the pamphlets.

It is difficult to talk of a plot in these two works, and, in *Féerie I* at least, it is even somewhat risky to even talk of a novel. A better term would be chronicle, a work of history written in the first person combining the perspective of the narrator with an enumeration of the events that the narrator has experienced, and accompanied by an analysis of the meaning of those events in the context of the larger drama. In *Féerie I,* the now familiar older narrator of the earliest works is on stage from the beginning of the work but he makes it immediately obvious that he is not chronicling the experiences of a mythical Ferdinand but rather of himself, Louis-Ferdinand Céline. He is convinced that the world has been turned upside down and that he, for the sake of the convenience of others, has been cast in the role of pariah and scapegoat. "Confusion of place and of time, ... it's a fairyland, you understand, yeah, a fairyland." [11] Of course this fairyland is seen ironically as something so weird and strange that it could not possibly exist at the present time, thus the addition of the "for another time" to the title.

He has been severely punished, this narrator, for he has been absent from France at the moment of his mother's death. Writing in exile, he longs to return to Paris's Père Lachaise cemetery to see her tombstone. His apartment has been sacked by members of the Résistance, whether Gaullists or not, and his papers scattered to the four winds. Seven whole manuscripts have been lost in the process. He hates Russia and Bolshevism as much as ever, but he also despises the United States, which he sees as being at least two centuries behind France in terms of culture.[12] But what did he do to merit such harsh treatment from his fellow citizens and why do all the other tenants in the apartment house where he lives in the rue Gaveneau (transposition of 4, rue Girardon where Céline actually had lived before his flight in 1944), hate him so much? Why, at the beginning of *Féerie I* do Marcel Arlon, his wife Clémence, and their son, who is studying law, come to visit Céline? The year seems to be 1944 and they never announce to him why they are there. But if we believe our narrator, they have come simply to see the death element in him — for to their mind he will soon be dead. Indeed, the visit of these three people to Céline's apartment at the beginning of the novel is only one of two elements in the whole work that can really be called fictional.

The other is the appearance of the legless cripple, Jules, who lost his legs in the battle of the Marne in 1914. He can thus lay claim, like Céline, to being a real Frenchman, for if there is one thing that Céline is proud of, it is his being a veteran of the fighting of 1914 in which he was severely wounded and for which he was later declared seventy percent incapacitated. But this legless creature, who is an artist by trade, will soon become an enemy of Céline, for he boldly calls the latter a German sympathizer in front of other people and then goes so far as to even seduce Céline's wife Lili/Arlette at the end of the novel. In other words, the fictional people who appear at the beginning of *Féerie I* come to see Céline before he dies. He has not fled from Paris yet — he will wait until June 1944 when the Allies are already at Rouen in Normandy to do so — but they sense and surely hope that he will die. But, as we know from reading this novel, he has not died, and the desire of the ironically named Clémence Arlon and her family will not be realized. Nor will he be dead by the end of the work, but at the same time he will be horribly disgraced and dishonored by the fact that one of his own, a true Frenchman like Jules, will seduce his wife and publicly rebuke him repeatedly. Granted that Céline finds Jules to be a hateful individual and that he does almost everything in his power to paint him as an unsavory person — he has a pornographic mind, is a drunkard, and is an "artist" mainly because he seems to be able to get his hands on nude models this way — we ought to recall that this portrait is nonetheless not far removed from the image of the average Frenchman that Céline had painted for us in the pamphlets. The taunts and insults they hurl back and forth at each other, not to mention the insults tossed at Céline by unidentified enemies, represent the writer's ostracism. Others want no part of him, and for that matter, despite the protestations of love that come from his wife, we even suspect that she — at least the fictional Lili/Arlette — is unhappy with him.

Perhaps the only point worth retaining in this unfortunate book are the few words mentioned by Céline toward the close of the volume where, inevitably, he talks of his style. Here, instead of calling it a "telegraphic" style as he had at the beginning of *Guignol's Band*, he refers to it as his "digest" style.[13] Clearly referring to the condensation practiced by the *Reader's Digest*, he goes on to say that since contemporary readers are in so much of a hurry and can no longer be counted on to sit down and read one hundred pages of text, his prose is designed to be read in bits of thirty pages at a time. Of course, we wonder how he can say this after having made us read through three hundred rather tedious pages of prose. The answer, if there is one, is most likely that

Céline felt his contribution to be a restructuring of the sentence, not of the novel. If his novels run on to seemingly interminable lengths (*Féerie I* and *II* run to about seven hundred pages), this is because he does not seem to be concerned with an overall organic structure in these later works but rather in a "musique" in each individual line.

Normance: Féerie ... II, is in some ways radically different from *Féerie I*. Whereas the latter is reminiscent of the pamphlets, the former reminds us of the more irrational elements in *Guignol's Band*. It differs too in that here in *Féerie II* what seems to be a plot can be followed — however tenuously — throughout the text, whereas *Féerie I* seems primarily to be a polemical work of self-justification. At the beginning of *Féerie II* the narrator, more like the older narrator of *Guignol's Band* than the direct presence of Céline himself encountered in *Féerie I*, falls down the elevator shaft of his apartment building. The seven flight fall shakes him up but, says he, this is really nothing for he has been knocked about a good deal since 1914. Jules reappears briefly at the beginning of the novel, but his character is never developed. Instead, a neighbor, M. Normance, a huge carcass of a man weighing somewhere between one hundred sixty and two hundred kilos is introduced. The ridiculously huge beast of a man can be taken to represent, in Céline's dream world, all those patients who forever came to him for medical advice, for Normance's main preoccupation seems to be to get the narrator to bring assistance to his unconscious wife. His usual method of getting Céline to help him is to simply plop his bulky mass on the body of the crippled doctor who has already bled for his country in the previous war.

Once again, the year seems to be 1944 and all Montmartre, then the rest of Paris, is undergoing a bombardment. Most of the narrator's building is destroyed in the process and some of the scenes of destruction evoke snatches of action that Céline will use again in the later chronicles. Here, though, the brute experience of the flight of 1944 - 45 is transposed back into a French setting in which the Parisians are being bombed by the Germans. Jules, if he is considered as a kind of everyman who is forever in disaccord with Céline, seems to welcome the bombers. Somehow scrambling to the top of a windmill, he can be seen directing planes over the city. Like so many of those other well-intentioned Frenchmen, at least at one point in their life (we recall that in 1914 Jules did his duty and lost his legs in the process), Jules is really a traitor because he has not listened to the narrator who had warned of this war for years. Jules is thus a metaphor for all those Frenchmen who unwittingly brought destruction upon their nation and who, unable to run away from their own defeat, ended up collaborating with the enemy. But Jules is not the only person who hates the narrator and who wants to destroy him, for all the neighbors we meet in the course of the book also seem to share this desire. After being knocked unconscious by these people early in the novel, Céline encounters another group of them later on — but here he wisely uses them for his own ends. Getting them to use Normance's body as a kind of battering ram to knock down a locked door (we recall once again the death of Van Claben in *Guignol's Band* who is also bounced on his head after being choked), the behemoth is disposed of.

But soon another mob of angry Frenchmen arrives in search of the narrator who is saved by his friend Ottavio. The latter carries him upstairs to what is left of his apartment. Searching for water, Ottavio knocks a hole in the wall allowing entry into the building next door where they meet the famous actor, Norbert, sitting silently in formal attire at a fully set table. Reminiscent of Céline's Fascist friend and travelling companion, the actor Le Vigan, this person, like many of the Frenchmen of his particular political persuasion before the war, is oblivious to where his own attitude was leading his nation. Norbert, we learn, is all dressed up because he is waiting for the Pope, for Churchill, and for Roosevelt, and in this he reminds us of those Fascists who hoped that by the intervention of the Pope, Germany could sign a separate peace treaty with the United States and England in order to continue the war against Communism. But Norbert, like those deluded Nazis and their fellow travellers, is in a dream world. As he sits there waiting in vain, the novel ends with sheets of paper seen falling upon the street below. It is the narrator's work that is being cast to the winds. France has been liberated and the war is about to end.

The dedications of these two volumes of *Féerie* are interesting. The first volume, dedicated "To Animals, To Sick People and To Prisoners," is symptomatic of that misanthropic Céline, who prepared this text for publication in 1951 and 1952. As he was to say later in *Nord*, when he stated that he had done the impossible in getting left and right, Monarchists and Communists, to agree on one thing, that he was "the greatest scum alive," [14] so also Céline cannot bring himself to find any kinship except with animals of which he usually had a goodly number in his household; the ill, whom he had cared for all his adult life; and prisoners, with whom at the time he shared a close bond. Written from this antisocial attitude it is no wonder that *Féerie I* is so heavily weighted down with long rambling pages that do nothing but test the ability of the reader to plod through. It is for this reason that in the final analysis the book is a failure as a novel and can be of interest ultimately only to the most inveterate Céline enthusiast. To us it seems to continue the I-told-you-so attitude of *Les Beaux draps*, for while it condemns the political conduct and ideological position of virtually everybody else in France during the war, this chronicle-*mémoire* argues strongly on behalf of the innocence of the narrator, who is presented as an innocent scapegoat.

Féerie II is dedicated to both Pliny the Elder and Gaston Gallimard. What at first sight might seem a bit strange can be explained when we recall that Pliny, like Céline, was the witness to a giant catastrophe, the eruption of Vesuvius, which was also responsible for his death. We can easily see why Céline, with his personal view of contemporary politics, chose to dedicate the book to him. The dedication underscores the whole "innocent bystander" theme of the novel, an idea that Céline would cling to for the rest of his life. Normance, the fat, stuffed, materialistic, and unimaginative *bourgeois* who is forever trying to get Ferdinand to give medical treatment to his wife, and who has also given his name to *Féerie II*, is the one who is principally at fault for Ferdinand's isolation. Their ability to communicate is virtually nonexistent and the fault, implies Céline, is not his but Normance's. Of course, Jules and Norbert are also movers and victims of the war, but it is Normance who, like all the rest of the neighbors, is the real enemy — and thus it is only fitting that he should be done away with by his own kind of people, a mob of common, ordinary, mindless Frenchmen. Céline, the innocent bystander, would have us believe that all he wanted to do was warn his fellow citizens of the impending catastrophe and for that he was almost killed. This at least is the underlying idea of the whole novel.

The second dedication of *Féerie II*, the one to Gaston Gallimard, can be explained by Céline's gratitude, at least at the time, to Gallimard for offering him a contract when no one would touch his work. It took courage to do that, and Gallimard fearlessly acted on Céline's behalf. Although Céline would complain in later years that the Gallimard house was a gang of thieves and that Gaston had cheated him out of money, the impulse to express gratitude here seems genuine. On the other hand, given a contract that obliged him to publish in the future in order to earn his advances, Céline went ahead and produced in *Féerie I* and *Féerie II* two books that can easily be considered his weakest. They ramble on endlessly and make almost no attempt at developing either plot or character. After seven hundred pages of this "telegraphic" or "digest" style, the reader's ability to keep interested is severely taxed. Pulverizing almost completely the traditional sentence in these two books, he has substituted for it an endless chain of small units of words, many of which contain no verb and which are linked either by the three dots or by exclamation points. Céline's longtime friend and political defender Albert Paraz has also defended Céline's claim to want to write a "digest" style in *Normance*. In a letter to a friend in 1954, shortly after the appearance of *Normance*, Paraz wrote: "For *Normance*, you are wrong to try to read it like a novel. It is an apocalypse. Take the Bible and read it, you will see that one cannot read it all at one time. You have to savor *Normance* page by page. And believe me, Céline could have written a sequel to *Guignol's Band* if he had wanted to. He sought another mode of expression, which is his artistic right." [15]

With the benefit of hindsight, and now being able to look at the whole Céline corpus, we can say that Paraz, first of all, had no way of knowing that the sequel to *Guignol's Band* was still in existence in 1954 or in fact that it had ever been written in the first place. As for his claim that Céline here in *Féerie* is seeking a new style, a new means of expression, this just does not stand up to an analysis of the two volumes. As we pointed out above, if anything, the books contain some of the worst aspects of both the pamphlets and *Guignol's Band*. The venom, bad faith, and intolerance shown toward political enemies in the pamphlets are still in evidence in these two books, and the refusal to develop plot and character, relying instead on verbal fireworks to sustain interest for over seven hundred pages, ultimately fails to sustain the reader's interest. Finally, given the overall weakness of *Féerie*, it is not too difficult to understand how the general indifference to Céline in literary circles just after the war could continue into the early fifties.

Guignol's Band after all, had been published under the Occupation, and for this reason it was not as widely read as perhaps it should have been. Thus, by the middle fifties Céline had become in the minds of many critics the aging and sickly author of two great books (*Voyage* and *Mort*) that were symptomatic of the early and middle thirties. His later work, in large part owing to its utter incomprehensibility, continued to be either deliberately ignored or simply unread. Given the self-righteous tone and hybrid form of the two volumes of *Féerie*, it is difficult to fault contemporary critics for largely failing to be impressed by these works.

III Entretiens avec le professeur Y
(Conversations with Professor Y)

At several points in *Féerie I* and *II* the narrator expresses the hope that people will buy his book. Alluding to Gaston Gallimard's possible exploitation of his impecunious situation, he implies not only that a high rate of sale will help him, but also that selling copies is what interests him most. Again, in *Entretiens avec le professeur Y* (1955), he comes right out and states that he has no terrible affection for Gaston Gallimard, his publisher, not because he thinks the latter is exploiting him, but because he is wealthy. Taking once again the position he had first espoused in *Voyage* and later in the pamphlets, he speaks here as a representative of those who must work every day to make ends meet, whereas Gallimard, independently wealthy, is not obliged to do so. Even Jean Paulhan, who had helped him during his exile by publishing a fragment of *Casse-Pipe* in the *Nouvelle Revue Francaise* at a time when Céline's name was anathema, is criticized here because he is at least wealthy enough to have a maid. Even the imagined interviewer, Professor Y, benefits from substantial financial resources, whereas Céline, still proud of his patriotic service in the front lines in 1914, has virtually nothing. He thus mocks Gallimard throughout this slim volume by repeatedly asking Professor Y how many pages have been filled up so far and by reminding us that the only reason he is consenting to the imagined interview in the first place is that Gallimard wants to stimulate discussion about his work — presumably to help sell more copies. Even the fictional interviewer, an ambitious academician whose manuscript is being read by someone else at Gallimard, is mocked repeatedly, for he is the only person who would consent to interview the century's greatest outsider.

In the course of the interview Céline dismisses all his contemporaries, while reserving a special dislike for Mauriac, whom he claims to have met once. Since the latter made a good deal of money as a writer, had his famous column in the *Figaro* for years, and was elected to the French Academy, he represents quite nicely all that Céline dislikes about official French literary life. Mauriac is thus dismissed as an idiot who seemed to Céline to have been lobotomized. Read by professors, his writings incorporated into school curricula, and typical of most writers who, like him, remain on the surface of things, Mauriac is different from Céline. As for himself, Céline claims that he has done for the novel in the twentieth century what the Impressionists did for painting in the nineteenth century: he has restored emotion to literature. Asserting that he is responsible for an invention that consists simply in endowing written language with emotion,[16] he points out that just as photography killed off traditional pre-Impressionist art, the cinema has put the traditional novel to death. But his invention has saved the novel, he claims, because it uses many of the tricks of cinema.[17] He does not elaborate on what these effects are, but he presumably means the quick cutting and fading of scenes without any transitional descriptions, the use of slang and everyday speech much like that used in the movies, and what he would like to believe is the emotional impact that his books have on the reader in comparison to ordinary novels that do not use his techniques. It is debatable and in fact doubtful that his books do reproduce the same kind or depth of emotional reactions as the cinema can, with the exception of course of *Voyage*.

Céline likens his writing to a subway as opposed to a bus. The inspiration came to him to become a writer who would try to put emotion into spoken language at a time when, just having begun his medical practice and living in Montmartre, he took the subway train across the city every day, from Pigalle to Issy. He chose the subway despite the fact that the same trip could be made by bus, a ride which, all things considered, had its advantages, for one could see any number of interesting and original people and happenings by remaining on the surface of things. But he chose the subway because it took him directly to his goal, and to him the heart of writing was the need to implant an emotional power in written language. Continuing his use of the comparison to the subway, he claims that in using his subway technique he carried along with him everything that the ordinary person would see on the surface, and for this reason his subway cars were packed to capacity. Thus, in order to keep the train on the tracks, he had to invent the system of the three little points, which he likens to the ties on a railroad track.[18] Thanks to this invention, writing had finally been liberated, just as music, painting, and architecture had been liberated generations earlier. And just as the Impressionists decided to do what a photographer could never do, that is, depict the artist's reaction to a flower as opposed to simply reproducing the flower, Céline too considers himself a literary Impressionist who, in forever using the first person point of view in his novels, can also rightly be called a lyricist.[19] As for those who dismiss him as someone who depends solely on the shock value of using slang and vulgarity to impress readers, he responds that such language to him is only a kind of pimento that can seduce a reader but cannot be expected to retain his interest for very long. For the simple reason that one must increase the dose of spices in order to continue to get the same effect, Céline claims that he early rejected an overreliance on slang in his work. Slang has its role in creating emotion in written language, but it is only a means and not an end.[20] The true end of his writing is the following: to create in the reader's mind the impression that as he reads a Céline book, someone else (presumably Céline himself) is reading to him within his head. Not reading in his ear as it were, but "in the intimacy of his nerves! ... right in his nervous system! in his very head!"[21] and this, he claims is "le secret de l'Impressionnisme." [22]

Significantly, Céline makes no claim, as usual, to being a thinker. His trick, his discovery, his invention, as far as he is concerned, is a technical one that has enabled the novel to go on living. He also claims that it is an invention that many other novelists — he names no names — have taken for their own ends, but always with discretion. Also of interest with regard to his technique is his assertion that even though he wanted to capture spoken language in writing he never resorted to the use of a dictaphone, which he categorically rejects as a mechanical intervention in the act of creation.

It can be said that *Féerie I* and *II* form, when added to *Entretiens*, a kind of trilogy, for all three are in one sense the result of Céline's need to publish after his return from captivity. Gaston Gallimard had supported him when his books no longer earned money and when the future was anything but bright. In return, as Céline states quite bluntly in *Entretiens*, Gallimard wanted him to write so that people would start talking about him again. On the other hand, we know from Céline's correspondence as well as from his other books and from the facts of his life (e.g., the hiding of his fortune in Denmark before World War II), that Céline always retained a kind of peasant cunning with respect to money and was forever lamenting that he never had enough of it because those who were in a position to do so were taking what rightfully belonged to him. As usual, we have to take his exaggerated claims with a grain of salt, but not reject them completely. As for his *ars poetica*, we have as good and as complete a statement of it in *Entretiens* as we can find in all of his published work. But this does not mean that it is complete. In his correspondence with Milton Hindus and his chats with Robert Poulet he also discussed the same subjects, and these sources, among others, must be consulted by any reader interested in learning what Céline thought about his own work. Finally, we cannot take him too seriously when he claims, by his innovative style, to have rendered the cinema obsolete. He may have borrowed some techniques from the cinema and put them to work in his novels, but when he claims that his style has made even the cinema a thing of the past,[23] we must chalk this up to the same kind of exaggeration we find in his rejection of all writers who use a language other than French.[24] The cinema was always one of his favorite targets, just as American writers were — and in his rejection of all foreign writers and languages in *Entretiens* his reference to Americans is only thinly veiled. Remembering that Céline in the pamphlets had considered the cinema to be the Jewish art par excellence, and the United States the greatest stronghold of international Jewry, we should not be surprised at these jibes.

CHAPTER 6

The Trilogy of Flight

I D'un château l'autre (Castle to Castle)

W HEN Céline published *D'un château l'autre* in 1957, he made it rather clear throughout the text that he was continuing to write in part because he had to do so in order to go on living. The few patients he was seeing by this time in his private practice did not generate enough income to keep life and limb together, nor did the money his wife earned from her dance lessons enable them by itself to make ends meet. For this reason Céline abandons any attempt in *D'un château l'autre* to hide his displeasure at his economic state and devotes a good deal of energy in the opening part of the book to castigating both Gaston Gallimard (whom he refers to as Achille Brottin) and Gallimard's editor Jean Paulhan (under the name of Loukoum) for pushing him to write in order to earn the advances he is presumably receiving from the firm. Since they want him to be humorous and to make people laugh as only he can, Céline makes a few half-hearted attempts at humor in this volume but they do not succeed. The bitter reminiscences of an aged and broken pariah are not very funny.

If there is a structure to this long rambling work, whose main interest might very well be that it tells us something about what life was like at Sigmaringen during the closing days of the war while the remains of Pétain's government took refuge there, it can be said to be built around the interplay of past and present, the bitterness of memories associated with the narrator's actions just prior to and during the war, and the harvest of misery that those actions have brought to him in his old age. Although by this time Céline was quite penniless, and — if one were to believe him completely — coldly exploited by Gallimard and Paulhan, this was so because all the money he had earned before the war was taken from him by his enemies.[1] In addition to the loss of money, he had also lost valuable manuscripts,[2] and had had his other possessions taken when his apartment in Montmartre was looted at the time of the liberation of Paris. And even as he writes this book, thinking back on his past and forward to his own death, he seems to regret that his mother does not even have her name on her gravestone in Paris's Pére-Lachaise Cemetery for fear that her son's enemies might come and deface it. One wonders then, and rightly so, will Céline himself be hounded by his enemies even after his death or is he just exaggerating?

In addition to disliking Gallimard and Paulhan, Céline also expresses his hatred for Mauriac and Claudel, whom he dismisses as weaklings. But his rejection of these two writers is nothing next to the venom that is reserved for Roger Vailland and Jean-Paul Sartre. Vailland, we recall, occasionally attended, starting in 1942, meetings of Résistance members in the apartment located right underneath Céline's. And since Vailland once stated that he could have, and probably should have, killed Céline during the war, Céline now challenges him to come and do battle. These reminiscences are quixotic and pathetic, but they reveal the deep wounds that were made on Céline's psyche by his rejection by just about everyone. His repeated denunciation of Sartre, who claimed that Céline had been a paid agent of the Germans during the war, is nothing less than virulent, especially since the influence of Céline on Sartre the novelist is almost everywhere apparent in the latter's first important novel, *La Nausée* (1938). [4] It is especially annoying to Céline to have been defamed by someone who owed him so much as an artist and who, as a successful playwright during the Occupation, had his plays performed with the approbation of the occupying Nazis.

At the outset of this work, which ought not to be called a novel, Céline is at home in Meudon and is generally annoyed with everyone. As mentioned above, he has had trouble with his editor and publisher and keeps going over his past wounds, both physical and psychological. But all the while, Céline is poking fun at himself for writing this text. He is forever counting the number of pages completed, piling them up seemingly against his will, but knowing all the time that Gallimard will accept nothing less. Then a narrative of kinds begins after about seventy-five pages of text, when he goes down near the Seine which passes through Meudon to make a house call on a patient named Mme. Niçois. After checking on her condition — she seems to have cancer — he dresses her wounds and gives her an injection of morphine. Then as he waits for her to drop off to sleep he gazes out the window and sees a *bateau-mouche*, one of those long, low, fleeting boats that ferry tourists up and down the Seine beneath the bridges of Paris. Named *La Publique*, it pulls up alongside the riverbank, and after a while Le Vigan, the actor friend of Céline who had accompanied him from Paris in 1944, gets off the boat with his Argentine wife Anita and a fellow named Emile who had been a member of the *Légion des Volontaires Français*, the rather sizable group of French Fascists that fought with distinction on the Eastern front against the Russians until the very end of the war.

After another thirty pages or so we learn that these characters and the boatman in command of *La Publique* are all figments of Céline's imagination, but now instead of invoking "delirium" as the source of this vision, the aging Céline prefers to talk about his past injuries and illnesses as the source of this kind of scene. Specifically, he states that the weird vision to which he has just treated us is the result of the dose of malaria he had contracted in the Cameroons in 1917.[5] As with the delirium attacks in his earlier work, this malaria attack also bears creative fruit since through it he begins to come to grips with the real story he has to tell, the tale of Sigmaringen. The visions of past and present are scrambled in his mind. He is in a cold sweat, his temperature is dangerously high, and his mind seems about to explode, but he knows that he must write even though he had made up his mind "not to write any more ... the very word 'writing' has always struck me as indecent! ... pretentious, narcissistic, 'have you read me?' ... that was my reason, the only one."[6] But for motives that are both financial and psychological (he exaggerates the former and barely mentions the latter although in our view this latter reason comes more and more to the fore in these last three books), he must take pen in hand and write. The fever passes, the sweats subside, he is able to relax. The verbal fireworks are suddenly ended, and now he begins the story of life in Sigmaringen as he remembers it — and transposes it — for his reader.

There is no attempt at a chronological reconstruction of events in *D'un château l'autre*, although in this volume Céline admits that he is writing essentially as a "mémorialiste."[7] He does mention a trip north to Berlin, but for the most part he is concerned with his memories of Pétain, Laval, various other Frenchmen of lesser note, and assorted Germans whom Céline met during the latter part of 1944 and early months of 1945 at Sigmaringen. He draws a few comic pages from the effect that certain German foods and beers had on the bowel movements of the people who lived in the same hotel in which he resided, for the one bathroom in the establishment was located on the second floor across from his room. But these pages and other attempts at humor seem forced, for underneath Céline's stoic veneer the reader senses a deep bitterness. In the end, the one impression we get of that particular time and place in history is one of complete delirium. With destruction on all sides of the town and Allied planes flying at will over Germany, Sigmaringen is still not bombed. The local gentry do not get along very well with each other and most of them are not even Nazis. Furthermore, all the Germans in the novel, whether wellborn or common people, resent having these fleeing Frenchmen in their midst occupying the Hohenzollern Castle. The future of each of the 1142 political refugees is precarious at best, and, as Céline himself lets us know, he would have four years of imprisonment, including eight months of solitary confinement, ahead of him in Denmark. The Danes would have preferred — as does everyone else he suspects — to have their Céline problem solved by just having him die in prison. But since he did not die, he is now telling his story before it is too late.

Perhaps the two strongest personal perceptions that one gets from this book are that Céline's racial consciousness had not really changed at all by 1957, and that he had come to realize over the years that *Voyage* was his greatest book. As for the first point, while he now no longer lashed out at Jews, he was as conscious as ever of the dominant dominating nature of genes. Taking the wife of one of the local German personalities at Sigmaringen, a certain Aïsha von Raumnitz who is of Lebanese origin (having met her husband while he served as a military attaché, presumably in Beirut, before the war), he expresses wonder at the beauty of her daughter in view of the fact that the girl has non-Aryan blood in her. "Speaking as a clinician, embryologist, and racist," he is astounded that their union "should have produced so beautiful a child!"[8] But this is not the only instance in the book where he permits himself such an observation. And in fact, as he wrote his

next two books, both of which are chronicles like this one, the
racial consciousness that Céline most likely always possessed would
express itself with more and more frequency.

The other thing that strikes the reader in this book is the
awareness that Céline had by this time, that his greatest and most
important book was *Voyage*. All the talk about the "three little
dots" notwithstanding, the book he wrote before this particular
stylistic wrinkle became the hallmark of his writing is the one for
which he knew he would be remembered. He had stated in
Entretiens avec le professeur Y, we recall, that his great contribution to Western letters in this century would be the
reproduction of the feeling of spoken language on the written page
— a feeling that the three little dots were supposed to help create.
In addition, he seemed to indicate in *Entretiens*, if only by
omission, that he was not a thinker, or a novelist with a definite
intellectual bent. But *Voyage*, to our mind at least, is his most
intellectual book, and it is also the one that is the most traditional
of his novels to read. The three dots do not dominate the text to the
point of distracting the reader, yet he does manage — and critics of
the book were the first to notice this aspect of it when it first appeared — to produce in the reader's mind the impression of seeing
spoken language on the printed page, even though the three dots
technique had not yet become all-pervading. Speaking of his
greatest book, he writes: "It's the *Voyage* that got me into all this.
... My most relentless persecutors date from the *Voyage*. ...
Nobody's forgiven me for the *Voyage*. ... It was the *Voyage* that
cooked my goose." [9] Or when he recalls that Gallimard now wants
him to write something funny, he realizes that "*Voyage* doesn't
seem so terribly funny to me. ... Altman didn't think it was funny
either ... or Daudet." [10] And this is so because Céline considers
himself, with *Voyage*, to be "the author of the first Communist
novel ever written ... they'll never write another! never! ... they
haven't got the guts!" [11] Never does he speak of his other books in
the same way, especially *Mort à crédit*, which some critics consider
his best book. Thus, at the very least, it is comforting to know that
such a tormenting and tormented writer was at least correct in
understanding which of his books was the one that would keep his
name alive for generations to come.

Céline returns to Meudon and to the present to conclude his
book. Waiting for his wife to come back from Paris, he hears

voices in the house and soon learns that his wife Lili has come in
with Mme. Niçois and another lady, named Mme. Armandine,
whom Mme. Niçois had met in the cancer ward at the hospital and
who now lives with her. Mme. Armandine has just had a breast
removed and, like so many of Céline's patients must have been
during his lifetime (we get a glimpse of some of them in *Voyage*),
she is outspoken and rude, calling Céline "stringbean" and telling
him she wants him to come and make a housecall on her and Mme.
Niçois that evening. The novel ends with Céline meekly going along
with her, agreeing to call later that evening, and underlining, as the
novel ends, this strange disproportion in his own character. The
same man who could write political pamphlets containing such
venom aimed at whole groups of humankind is here a weak and
passive man when confronted with one brash patient.

II   Nord (North)

Nord was written in the late fifties and published in 1960. Just as
Mort à crédit crossed back in time to a period in Ferdinand's life
that preceded the one described in *Voyage*, *Nord* treats the events
in Céline's wanderings that preceded his arrival in Sigmaringen in
late 1944 and that had already been described in *D'un château
l'autre*. Having left Paris in June 1944, he originally went to Baden
Baden and from there went north to Berlin and as far as the Baltic
coast in the hope of being able to escape to Denmark. When it
appeared that he would not be able to get out, and when the
political refugees from Vichy were evacuated by the Germans to
Sigmaringen, he was ordered to head south, a journey that took
him hundreds of miles from where he wanted to be, in order to
serve as doctor to the residents of the Hohenzollern Castle. *Nord*
deals with his sojourns at Baden Baden and Berlin, and then at
Rostock, Warnemünde, and Zornhof in the north during the
middle of 1944.

In this book, Céline is even more conscious of old age. He calls
himself a "chronicler," [12] and claims he is entitled to discard
chronology and to backtrack in time since the disorder in the *Reich*
during this period was so great. Going back to a device used earlier
in the two parts of *Féerie* and in *Entretiens*, but proportionately
less in *D'un château l'autre*, he employs an ironic questioner, a
kind of mocking "wise guy" who hoots at him from the audience,

reminding him during the opening twenty pages or so of the novel to get on with the tale and to stop boring his reader with his personal gripes. This technique has the effect of disarming the reader somewhat but it does not alter the fact that reading this book, like *D'un château l'autre*, is no easy proposition. It is tedious going, although its value as a historical chronicle is more evident than was the case with the earlier work. For whereas *D'un château l'autre* was forever getting bogged down in personal recriminations, such asides are less evident here (our guess is that they were removed by an editorial red pencil), and the reconstruction of events and personalities is more readily — although not easily — understandable.

Perhaps the best part of the book is the lengthy section devoted to the trip to Berlin, where Céline finds that whole sections of the city have already been bombed to the ground, but where, despite the rampant disorder, the citizens of the city have still piled the rubble up neatly outside their doors. His colleague, the madly francophile German doctor Harras, takes him to a Huguenot village nearby where, until a generation before, French had been spoken in the local area and where the village church dates back to 1695 — just a few years after Louis XIV revoked the Edict of Nantes. Later, while living in a village near the Baltic, Céline manages some funny pages with a group of Berlin prostitutes running wild in the area and the incongruous presence of a group of conscientious objectors doing nonmilitary work nearby. The local gentry in this region, the von Leidens, and the less distinguished Kretzers, are not very compelling people and Céline finds it difficult to sustain interest in their petty dislikes and manias. Although we learn that one of the von Leidens is a morphine addict, and that another one is morally depraved, we are relieved when the narrative breaks off. The novel ends with Céline and his entourage still in flight, travelling north toward Stettin.

In this book, just as in the earlier one, there are attacks against Gallimard, but the reader has grown used to that by now. What is more interesting, though, is Céline's silence when the faceless voice in his audience taunts him for having done nothing but live on his reputation since writing *Voyage*.[13] Having been "raised on sweat and boiled noodles,"[14] Céline argues strongly that he is a genuine son of the lower class by birthright. Calling himself an "anarchist"[15] in politics, he claims that "the real iron curtain is between

144 LOUIS-FERDINAND CÉLINE

the rich and the poor."[16] Just as *Voyage* originally got him into trouble for describing life as he saw it, so also *Les Beaux draps* was nothing more than a chronicle that described the situation his country was in just after the defeat of 1940. But since he belonged to the poor and powerless in society and not the rich and influential, he has been persecuted for what he wrote.[17] Serving as France's universal scapegoat, he makes people from all sides of the political spectrum feel good in hating him. But is that all, one wonders, that he has to say, as one puts down this book? Having taken us on a journey back in time past the days at Sigmaringen and left us suspended at book's end on a train going nowhere in particular, one puts down *Nord* with a feeling of incompleteness and of disappointment, for a great storyteller has obviously not finished telling his tale.

III   Rigodon (Rigadoon)

That sequel was finally published after Céline's death in *Rigodon*, the third book in this trilogy of flight which, according to its editor, was written during 1960 and 1961, but only published in 1969. After Céline told his wife on the morning of July 1, 1961, that the book was finally completed, he wrote a note to Gallimard informing him of the news. His work done, he then died later that evening and was buried in a quiet, private ceremony in the local cemetery before the news was released to the press.

The title of this volume, evoking a form of eighteenth century dance called the rigadoon in English, has a variety of meanings, each of which brings to completion the portrait that Céline wanted to leave of himself with posterity. As a dance the rigadoon is performed by a couple that moves across the floor briskly. Céline, a lifelong admirer of dance and of ballerinas, had, as we already know, married one. Thus, the rigadoon is a hymn to the other member of the couple, Lucette, who had remained faithful to him throughout years of bitterness and suffering and who had borne more than her share of mistreatment (we recall, for example that she too was imprisoned for a while in Denmark) at the hands of others. The rigadoon is also the dance of death. The last dance, so to speak, that Céline will be involved in. For not only is he conscious as he writes *Rigodon* that his health is failing and that this will be his last book, but also the subject matter of the volume, tracing the flight of the couple across a Germany in flames to an imprisonment in Denmark, touches everywhere on death — the end of the journey for Céline. The word rigadoon also evokes the notion of the music that is played to the accompaniment of the dance, and reminds one of the many times Céline had referred to his style as a music — his own, personal "petite musique" — that no one else could imitate. The word therefore brings to mind both the writer and his work, but it does not stop there. A final meaning of rigadoon refers to the slow, solemn beating of drums that in former times was used in the French army when offenders were being paraded before punishment. This last meaning evokes the image of the man himself that Céline wants to leave with us. Being punished by his fellow Frenchmen, the solitary loner he had always been (and it was a role he seemed to prefer) was conscious of his isolation from others right up until the end.

The narrative line in this third volume is even more disjointed than in the first two books, and at one point, when it takes Céline back from northern Germany to Sigmaringen a second time, from which point he then starts out on his successful journey to Denmark, it is clearly in contradiction with the actual chronology of events as he lived them — and even as they had been presented, however vaguely, in *D'un château l'autre* and *Nord*. As with the first two volumes, this one, too, begins with Céline in Meudon griping about his living conditions and poverty. Then, after about thirty pages, he takes us back in time to terminate the narrative he had suddenly broken off in *Nord*. He is on a flatcar going north from Berlin to the Baltic; then suddenly he is travelling south again, all the way to Sigmaringen. On the way, they meet a band of lepers accompanied by a nun and a Doctor Proseidon, and after going through Ulm and Augsburg, he arrives at Sigmaringen only to start out from there again — this time successfully — toward Denmark. Describing his trip toward the south, Céline writes some of his best pages in telling of the bombing attack that his train underwent and in the end successfully avoided by hiding under a mountain until the RAF went away. Verbal fireworks that rank with some of his better writing from earlier days are visible here in an otherwise tedious and disjointed narrative.

On his last trip northward he passes through a small town near Hanover where the Nazis herd a large group of refugees into a railroad station and then demolish the building with everyone inside. From here Céline gets on a flatcar travelling toward Hamburg, and once he arrives there safely he goes straight to the border, which he crosses without incident. Having hitched a ride on a Red Cross train carrying refugees to Sweden, he passes as a Red Cross doctor and makes it safely to Copenhagen where, he tells us, he had deposited six million francs in the Landsman Bank before the war.[18] Presumably this money — however much of it was actually there — was never turned over to him. The book ends with a sudden change of scene. We are back in Meudon and Céline is out of breath. His manuscript, he exaggerates slightly, is now 791 pages long and Gallimard should be happy with that. Then a visitor comes. It is Jean-A. Ducourneau, a Balzac scholar who has been entrusted by Gallimard with the task of editing Céline's first two novels for publication in the prestigious *Editions de la Pléiade*. Proud that this recognition is being given to him while he is still alive, a rare honor indeed, he tells us that *Voyage* is, in his opinion, "a date in history," and that everything that has been written since 1932 by anyone else is nothing but "clumsy imitation, lukewarm gook."[19]

This final recognition of the rock upon which his future reknown would be based is also accompanied at the very end of the novel by an expression of that other personal conviction that had been so strongly expressed in *Nord*. Speaking as the racially conscious creature he had always been, he laments what he takes to be the imminent takeover of France by the Chinese, an event that for him symbolizes the eventual and probably inevitable victory of dominant genes over recessive ones. All of France will become bastardized once the Chinese come because "it's only the blood that counts! they've got the 'dominant blood' ... and don't forget it!"[20] Having earlier reminded us that he is a "parasitologist! doctorated! don't forget it,'"[21] he then reaffirms his commitment to an essentially biological view of man: "I'm a biologist, I tell you, that's all ... only biology exists, the rest is hot air! ... all the rest ... the blacks and yellows always win! ... the whites are always the losers!"[22] It is for this reason — that is to say, because he views man essentially as a biological phenomenon first and foremost, as an animal with intelligence but as an animal nonetheless — that he rejects absolutely all religion, but especially Christianity, since organized religions tend to preach brotherhood and equality and to Céline there is nothing equal among races. In fact, as he sees it, all that the white race can gain by association with less pure strains is mongrelization — from which point total disappearance as a recognizable species is only a matter of time. For this reason too, he can say that "Europe died at Stalingrad," [23] when Hitler's armies suffered the defeat that turned out to be the turning point in the war on the eastern front. From that point on the white race has been on the decline, so there is no use in trying to save it at this late date. Of course Céline does not even mention Jews in these, the last pages he ever wrote, but one cannot help but conclude that his earlier obsessions had not left him. As usual, however, it is a matter of degree that one must take into consideration when evaluating his racial consciousness at the end of his life. Was his fear of the Yellow Peril as it is voiced in *Rigodon* only another more sly and sophisticated way of getting at Jews and other "orientals," or is it a politically neuter statement made by a man of science? In the final analysis we cannot be sure. While Céline had seen to it that his pamphlets of the thirties would never be published again, he still continued to be conscious of racial differences and to talk about them. The problem, of course, is that, given his past history, Céline is not just any ordinary biologist. His lamentable performance in the pamphlets will forever be a stumbling block to his critics, even his most sympathetic ones.

CHAPTER 7

Conclusion

A T this point it should be obvious that we consider *Voyage* to be among the greatest novels written in any language in this century. There is no need to repeat here the reasons why we esteem *Voyage* so highly, but there can be no doubt that its influence has been great on subsequent writers and will probably continue to be so. Significantly, this novel was written before Céline's mind became cluttered with bitterness and resentment in the late thirties, and it is thanks to this book that his legacy survives in the tragic vision of Beckett, in the imitation of him by Sartre, Queneau, and Genet among others, and in the admiration expressed for him by people like Le Clézio, Robbe-Grillet, and Barthes. In this country, of course, writers like Henry Miller, Jack Kerouac, Joseph Heller, Kurt Vonnegut, Jr., William Burroughs, and Ken Kesey owe an obvious debt to the author of *Voyage*.

At present Céline studies are just beginning to catch up with the immense body of work to be considered. If Céline's first two novels have been studied quite closely and admired by many for the last forty years, the same cannot be said about the works that were published after his return from Denmark. We do not by any means presume to have had the last word on *Féerie I* and *II*, *Pont de Londres*, or the three volumes that we refer to as the trilogy of flight: *D'un château l'autre*, *Nord*, and *Rigodon*. It seems to us that future research on Céline ought to address itself to these works to determine whether or not they have been judged too harshly. As for the pamphlets, we can see no reason to have them republished. With resolve and determination, the interested reader can always get his hands on them. As the years go by and the future unfolds, attitudes might change regarding Céline's role on the French political scene beginning in 1937. But be that as it may, the existence of the pamphlets will probably forever be a stumbling block to admirers of Céline's novels. If he had not written them, he might well be ranked today as second to none among modern French novelists, and many of those readers who admire his work would perhaps speak and write more forcefully on his behalf than they do now — if at all. But Céline would not have had it any other way. The dark journey of Doctor Destouches/Céline has ended. But the fictional transposition of that journey into the shadowy adventures of Bardamu/Robinson still provokes readers to follow behind him into the depths of the night of modern life.

Notes and References

Chapter One

1. Céline's father's family had originally come from Flanders, while his mother's family was of Breton stock. He would later emphasize this Breton connection as a contributing hereditary factor in his becoming a writer.

2. Louis Montourcy, "Monsieur Destouches," *L'Herne,* III (1963), 9 - 10.

3. *Ibid.,* p. 9. His father retired in 1923 at the age of fifty-eight. He died in 1932.

4. This is a difficult period in Céline's life to reconstruct. Erika Ostrowsky, in *Voyeur Voyant: A Portrait of Louis-Ferdinand Céline* (New York, 1971), does not even treat this period in his life. See Patrick McCarthy, *Céline* (New York, 1976), pp. 11 - 48.

5. Jean-A. Ducourneau, in the "chronologie" section of the Pléiade edition of *Voyage au bout de la nuit* and *Mort à crédit,* was among the first to point out that Céline was never trepanned. See Céline, *Voyage au bout de la nuit et Mort à crédit,* edited by Henri Mondor (Paris, 1962), p. xviii. See also Jean-A. Ducourneau, "La Fin d'une légende: Céline n'a jamais été trépanné," *Le Figaro Littéraire,* no. 1071 (27 octobre 1966), 4.

6. Georges Geoffroy, "Céline en Angleterre," *L'Herne*, III (1963), 11 - 12.

7. Published in Rennes by Francis Simon, 1924. It is interesting to note that Céline did not pick a laboratory research subject to deal with in his thesis. A controlled scientific exercise leading to objectively measurable results clearly did not interest him.

8. Max Dorian, "Céline rue Amélie," *L'Herne,* III (1963), 25 - 27.

9. See *Oeuvres de Louis-Ferdinand Céline,* éd. Jean-A. Ducourneau (Paris, 1966 - 69), 5 vols., I, 740 - 46.

10. Ostrowsky, pp. 395 - 96.

11. In the words of Jeanne Carayon, "un 'juge juif' la lui a 'soufflée,'" "Le Docteur écrit un roman," *L'Herne,* III (1963), 23.

12. Ostrowsky, pp. 68 - 84; see also Jacqueline Morand, *Les Idées politiques de Louis-Ferdinand Céline* (Paris, 1972), pp. 44 - 45; and Henri Mahé, *La Brinquebale avec Céline* (Paris, 1969), p. 102.

13. See Céline's thoughts on the subject in Jacques Darribehaude, "Le 'voyage' au cinéma," *L'Herne,* III (1963), 191 - 94.

14. Marcel Brochard, "Céline à Rennes," *L'Herne,* III (1963), 16 - 17.

15. Mahé, pp. 118 - 19; and "L.-F. Céline à Milton Hindus," *L'Herne,* V (1965), 104 - 105.

16. "L.-F. Céline à Milton Hindus," p. 104. See also: Ostrowsky, pp. 81 - 82, 100 - 110; and *D'un château l'autre* (*Oeuvres,* IV, 452).

17. Henri Mondor, ed., *Voyage au bout de la nuit et Mort à crédit* (Paris, 1962), p. xxiv.

18. See David O'Connell, "Eugéne Dabit: A French Working Class Novelist," *Research Studies,* XLI (1973), 217 - 33. See also André Gide, *Retour de l'U.R.S.S.* (Paris, 1936); and Pierre Herbart, *En U.R.S.S.S.,* (Paris, 1937).

19. Gen Paul, "Chez Gen Paul, à Montmartre," *L'Herne,* III (1963), 38. "Je m'amusais fort sachant que Céline, homme fin et pur, sans besoins, sans vice, sans voiture, sans servante, ne buvant que de l'eau et ne fumant pas, était un des très rares êtres sur lesquels on n'avait pas de prise. Un homme impossible à acheter."

20. It was revived again by the Théâtre de la Plaine in 1973 and reviewed by Claude Dubois, *Esprit,* no. 423 (avril 1973), 958 - 60; and by Philippe Sénart, *Revue des Deux Mondes* (avril 1973), 165 - 67.

21. Ostrowsky, pp. 97 - 99.

22. Morand, pp. 43 - 45. Other possible unfortunate experiences that Céline might have had with Jews are expressed by the allegations that: (1) a Jewish financier bilked him out of most of his earnings from his first two novels, which we consider highly unlikely since he himself admits in *Rigodon* (*Oeuvres,* V, 470), that he deposited about six million francs in a Danish bank before the war; (2) Jewish critics tried to end his career by criticizing *Mort à crédit,* which is unsubstantiated; (3) Jewish superiors at the League of Nations held him in check there, which is also unsubstantiated. We might also recall here that Elizabeth Craig seems to have married an American Jew, that his early ballets *Naissance d'une fée* and *Voyou Paul brave Virginie* were turned down by critics who happened to be Jewish and that *Voyage* was first read and rejected at Gallimard by a reader who also happened to be a Jew, Benjamin Crémieux. An objective observer can see that each of these incidents was purely coincidental, but Céline did not, or did not want to, see them that way.

Of course, even if all these allegations were true, they still would not justify Céline's later animosity against *all* Jews. But, set against the virulent anti-Semitism of the era, these incidents might have seemed to Céline's essentially vengeful and intolerant lower middle class mind like a pattern of events.

23. Lucien Rebatet, "D'un Céline l'autre, " *L'Herne,* III (1963), 45.

24. Robert Champfleury, "Céline ne nous a pas trahis," *L'Herne,* III (1963), 60 - 66.

25. Rebatet, p. 49.

26. *Ibid.,* III, p. 46, "Ils ont paumé, et nous avec. Une armée qui

n'apporte pas une révolution avec elle, dans les guerres comme celle-là, elle est cuite. Tordus, les Frizous."

27. *Ibid.*, pp. 53 - 54, Rebatet gives a slightly different version of the story, claiming that the money had been sent to a Dane working in Copenhagen as court photographer. This man allegedly converted the money to gold and buried it in his back yard. Céline himself tells us in *Rigodon* (*Oeuvres*, V, 470), that he had deposited the sum of six million francs in the Landsman Bank located on Peter Bang Wej at an unspecified date, presumably before the war.

28. It should be noted that virtually all of his German friends were, like himself, medical doctors. In addition to Harras, men like Epting, Haubolt, and Knapp fall into the same category. There is no proof that they were Gestapo agents.

29. Robert Aron, *Histoire de Vichy* (Paris: 1954), p. 723. The installation period took place during November 1944 and the period of hope extended from about December 1944 until April 1945 when, with the future looking bleak, the collaborators began to flee.

30. It is often difficult to know for sure when events took place in Céline's life. Here, for example, the Pléiade edition gives the date of arrest as December 20 (p. xxix). Erika Ostrowsky, in *Voyeur Voyant*, agrees (p. 397), but in her earlier work, *Céline and His Vision* (New York, 1967), she had offered the date of December 25 (p. 10). We follow Morand (p. 174) here and throughout this section.

31. The French government apparently succeeded in having Céline temporarily taken from the hospital and thrown back into prison on several occasions between February and June 1947.

32. Jean-Paul Sartre, "Portrait de l'antisémite," *Les Temps Modernes*, III (1945), 462. "Si Céline a pu soutenir les thèses socialistes des Nazis, c'est qu'il était payé. Au fond de son coeur, il n'y croyait pas. ..."

33. Ducourneau, p. xxix.

34. The two volumes of *L'Herne* devoted to Céline contain selections from these letters. A handy list of Céline's letters can be found in Allen Thiher, *Céline: The Novel as Delirium* (New Brunswick, 1972), pp. 259 - 60. The bulk of his correspondence remains in private hands and is largely unpublished.

35. Morand, pp. 195 - 200; and *L'Herne*, V (1965), 319 - 25.

36. Morand, p. 199. "*Première question:* Destouches Louis Ferdinand dit Louis Ferdinand Céline, accusé non présent, est-il coupable d'avoir en France, de 1940 à 1944, en tous cas entre le 16 juin 1940 et la date de la Libération, en temps de guerre, sciemment accompli des actes de nature à nuire à la Défense Nationale?

Deuxième question: L'action si-dessus spécifiée sous la question no. 1 a-t-elle été commise avec l'intention de favoriser les entreprises de toutes natures de l'Allemagne puissance ennemie de la France ou de l'une quelconque des puissances de l'Axe en guerre contre les nations alliées?"

37. Morand quotes these and others in reaction to the verdict, pp. 199 - 200.

38. Roger Nimier, "Donnez à Céline le Prix Nobel!" *Les Nouvelles Littéraires*, 18 septembre 1956, p. 1.

39. *L'Herne*, V (1965), 94, "Celte dans chaque pouce de ma misérable personne. .... le plus français celte des Français."

Chapter Two

1. Dorian, p. 26. As is usually the case with Céline, contradictory statements abound. Robert Poulet, *Non ami Bardamu: Entretiens familiers avec L.-F. Céline* (Paris, 1958), pp. 23 - 26, states that the manuscript arrived in the mail and that it was wrapped up with the text of another novel, the latter written by a woman who lived in Céline's apartment building.

2. Mondor, in the Pléiade edition, p. x. "A ce moment la vogue était aux populistes, dont Dabit que je connaissais un peu ... flèche de tout bois! ... 1932 ... je pris le prénom de ma mère, Céline, pour ne pas être repéré ..."

3. *Oeuvres*, I, 777 - 815. The collection of review articles of *Voyage* gathered here shows how the novel had a strong and generally positive effect on writers, critics, and intellectuals of both the left and right.

4. *Voyage*, Pléiade edition, p. x. Support by Daudet, whose earlier lobbying on behalf of both Proust and Bernanos had procured Goncourt prizes for them, should, in ordinary circumstances, have been sufficient to assure the prize's being awarded to Céline. His inability to succeed in this endeavor underlines the degree of hostility to the work that existed among the other members of the jury.

5. The *Carnet du cuirassier Destouches* (*Notebook of Cuirassier Destouches*) has been published in *L'Herne*, III (1963), 9 - 11.

6. Poulet, p. 6. "Le gars Eugéne Dabit avait récoulté un gros succés avec son *Hôtel du Nord*, où il avait fourré ses souvenirs d'enfance. Je me suis dit: "J'en ferais bien autant. Allons-y!""

7. *Ibid.*, p. 43. "Jamais je ne le dirai assez: mon intention, c'était de vendre quatre ou cinq mille exemplaires d'un bouquin vrai; les droits m'auraient fourni de quoi me loger décemment."

8. See: Milton Hindus, "Louis-Ferdinand Céline: Excerpts from his Letters," *Texas Quarterly*, V (1962), 26 - 27. A more complete edition of these letters was published in the original French in *L'Herne*, V (1965), 67 - 112.

9. All our quotes from *Voyage au bout de la nuit* are from the 1934 English translation of the work, *Journey to the End of the Night*, by John H. P. Marks (New York: New Directions, 1934; reprinted 1960), p. 7. "La guerre en somme c'était tout ce qu'on ne comprenait pas. Ca ne pouvait pas continuer." *Oeuvres*, I, 10

10. *Journey*, p. 15. "Quand on n'a pas d'imagination, mourir c'est peu

de chose, quand on en a, mourir c'est trop. Voilà mon avis. Jamais je n'avais compris tant de choses à la fois." *Oeuvres,* I, 16.

11. This novel, dealing with the historic battle of 1916, is contained in volumes 15 and 16 of Jules Romains, *Les Hommes de bonne volonté,* (Paris, 1932 - 47).

12. Sartre read closely and was surely influenced by *Voyage.* His fictional Bouville in *La Nausée* (1938) is evocative of Céline's Noirceur-sur-la-Lys. Allen Thiher, "Céline and Sartre," *Philological Quarterly,* L (1971), 292 - 305, has broken ground on the problem of the influence of *Voyage* on Sartre. More remains to be done on this question.

13. *Journey,* p. 56. "Alors je suis tombé malade, fiévreux, rendu fou, qu'ils ont expliqué à l'hôpital, par la peur. C'etait possible. La meilleure des choses à faire, n'est-ce pas, quand on est dans ce monde, c'est d'en sortir? Fou ou pas, peur ou pas." *Oeuvres,* I, 46.

14. *Journey,* p. 61. "Alors vivent les fous et les lâches!" *Oeuvres,* I, 50.

15. *Journey,* p. 170. "Tout est revenu ... Des années venaient de passer d'un seul coup. J'avais été bien malade de la tête, j'avais de la peine ... A présent que je savais, que je l'avais repéré, je ne pouvais m'empêcher d'avoir tout à fait peur. M'avait-il reconnu lui? En tout cas il pouvait compter sur mon silence et ma complicité" *Oeuvres,* I, 127.

16. Unfortunately, the description of these activities has been deleted from the Marks translation. Perhaps it should be mentioned here again that we need a good modern translation of *Voyage,* for the only one available is weakened both by an inability to express the power of Céline's prose and by the frustrating deletions of what must have seemed in 1934 like scandalous writing.

17. *Journey,* p. 183. "Je n'avais plus de délire." *Oeuvres,* I, 136.

18. *Journey,* p. 199. "La vérité, c'est une agonie qui n'en finit pas. La vérité de ce monde c'est la mort. Il faut choisir, mourir ou mentir. Je n'ai jamais pu me tuer moi." *Oeuvres,* I, 148.

19. "Et où aller dehors, je vous le demande, dès qu'on n'a plus en soi la somme suffisante de délire?" *Oeuvres,* I, 148.

20. *Journey,* p. 228. "J'avais même honte de tant de mal qu'elle se donnait pour me conserver. Je l'aimais bien, sûrement, mais j'aimais encore mieux mon vice, cette envie de m'enfuir de partout, à la recherche de je ne sais quoi, par un sot orgueil sans doute, par conviction d'une espèce de supériorité." *Oeuvres,* I, 169.

21. *Journey,* p. 235. "Bonne, admirable Molly, je veux si elle peut encore me lire, d'un endroit que je ne connais pas, qu'elle sache bien que je n'ai pas changé pour elle, que je l'aime encore et toujours, à ma manière." *Oeuvres,* I, 174.

22. *Journey,* p. 235. "...pour devenir soi-même avant de mourir." *Oeuvres,* I, 174.

23. *Journey,* p. 235. "J'avais de la peine, de la vraie, pour une fois, pour

tout le monde, pour moi, pour elle, pour tous les hommes." *Oeuvres*, I, 174.

24. *Journey*, p. 268. "On me retirera difficilement de l'idée que si ça m'a repris ça n'est pas surtout à cause de Robinson. ... De le rencontrer à nouveau, Robinson, ça m'avait donc donné un coup et comme une espèce de maladie qui me reprenait." *Oeuvres*, I, 198.

25. *Journey*, p. 332. "Etre riche, c'est une autre ivresse, c'est oublier. C'est même pour ça qu'on devient riche, pour oublier." *Oeuvres*, I, 245.

26. *Journey*, p. 241. "Sur sa face livide dansotait cet infini petit sourire d'affection pure que je n'ai jamais pu oublier. Une gaîté pour l'univers." *Oeuvres*, I, 179.

27. *Journey*, p. 305. "Parce que, tu vois, les hommes quand ils sont bien portants, y a pas à dire, ils vous font peur ... Surtout depuis la guerre ... Moi je sais à quoi ils pensent ... Ils s'en rendent pas toujours compte eux-mêmes ... Mais moi, je sais à quoi ils pensent ... Quand ils sont debout, ils pensent à vous tuer ... Tandis que quand ils sont malades, y a pas à dire ils sont moins à craindre ... Faut t'attendre à tout, que je te dis, tant qu'ils tiennent debout. C'est pas vrai? *Oeuvres*, I, 225.

28. *Journey*, p. 306. "En cherchant, je me rendis compte qu'il avait peut-être raison Robinson." *Oeuvres*, I, 225.

29. *Journey*, p. 352. "Vivre tout sec, quel cabanon! La vie c'est une classe dont l'ennui est le pion, il est là tout le temps à vous épier d'ailleurs, il faut avoir l'air d'être occupé, coûte que coûte, à quelque chose de passionnant, autrement il arrive et vous bouffe le cerveau. Un jour, qui n'est rien qu'une simple journée de 24 heures c'est pas tolérable. Ça ne doit être qu'un long plaisir presque insupportable une journée, un long coït une journée, de gré ou de force." *Oeuvres*, I, 259.

30. *Journey*, p. 368. "Le souvenir de Robinson revenait me tracasser." *Oeuvres*, I, 270.

31. *Journey*, p. 392. "Je ne l'écoutais plus. Il me décevait et me dégoûtait un peu pour tout dire. 'T'es bourgeois' que je finis par conclure (Parce que pour moi y avait pas pire injure à cette époque). Tu ne penses en définitive qu'à l'argent ... Quand tu reverras clair tu sera devenu pire que les autres!" *Oeuvres*, I, 287.

32. *Journey*, p. 393. "Ils en ont des pitiés les gens, pour les invalides et les aveugles et on peut dire qu'ils en ont de l'amour en réserve. Je l'avais bien senti, bien des fois, l'amour en réserve. Y en a énormément. On peut pas dire le contraire. Seulement c'est malheureux qu'ils demeurent si vaches avec tant d'amour en réserve, les gens. Ça ne sort pas, voilà tout. C'est pris en dedans, ça reste en dedans, ça leur sert à rien. Ils en crèvent en dedans, d'amour." *Oeuvres*, I, 288.

33. *Journey*, p. 395. "... et je me suis lancé dans une définition de son caractère à Robinson, comme si je le connaissais, moi son caractère, mais je me suis aperçu tout de suite que je ne connaissais guère Robinson ..." *Oeuvres*, I, 289.

34. Unfortunately, space does not allow us to discuss this scene, in which Robinson, Bardamu, and Madelon are attracted to a yacht docked by the river bank by the singing of a song that only underlines the main theme of the novel: "Ferme tes jolis yeux, car les heures sont brèves au pays merveilleux, au doux pays du rêve. Ferme tes jolis yeux car la vie n'est qu'un songe, l'amour n'est qu'un mensonge, ferme tes jolis yeux." *Oeuvres*, I, 291 - 92. In this scene Céline pokes fun at the *bourgeois* artist who invites them aboard his boat. Is this man's art, which is mild, innocuous, and ultimately vapid, real art, or is the kind that Céline the author is engaging in real? Is Bardamu's approach to life real, or is it invalid in comparison to that of Robinson?

35. *Journey*, p. 439. "N'avez-vous pas toujours entretenu d'excellents rapports avec notre clientèle?" *Oeuvres*, I, 320.

36. *Journey*, p. 460. "Moralement, nous n'étions pas à notre aise. Trop de fantômes, par-ci, par là." *Oeuvres*, I, 335.

37. *Journey*, p. 473. "'Flac! Flac!' Je lui ai collé deux gifles à étourdir un âne." *Oeuvres*, I, 344.

38. *Journey*, p. 501. "Mais il n'y avait que moi, bien moi, moi tout seul, à côté de lui, un Ferdinand bien véritable auquel il manquait ce qui ferait un homme plus grand que sa simple vie, l'amour de la vie des autres. De ça, j'en avais pas, ou vraiment si peu que c'était pas la peine de le montrer. J'étais pas grand comme la mort moi. J'étais bien plus petit. J'avais pas la grande idée humaine moi." *Oeuvres*, I, 363.

39. *Journey*, p. 505. "C'était pas à envisager que je parvienne jamais moi, comme Robinson, à me remplir la tête avec une seule idée mais alors une superbe pensée tout à fait plus forte que la mort ..." *Oeuvres*, I, 366.

40. *Journey*, p. 509. "... qu'on n'en parle plus." *Oeuvres*, I, 369.

41. Walter Orlando, "Grandeurs et misères de Bardamu," *La Table Ronde*, LVII (September 1952), 172. "Une oeuvre originale dont l'influence s'exerce trop tôt finit par se fondre dans sa propre postérité."

42. J. H. Matthews, "Céline's *Journey to the End of Night*," *Contemporary Review*, no. 1095 (March 1957), 160.

43. Kingsley Widmer, "The Way Down to Wisdom of Louis-Ferdinand Céline," *Minnesota Review*, VIII (1968), 91.

44. *Ibid.*, p. 90.

45. "L.-F. Céline à Milton Hindus," *L'Herne*, V (1965), 92. "J'ai été élevé tout naturellement en catholique — baptême, première communion, mariage à l'église, etc. (comme 38 millions de Français). La foi? hum! c'est autre chose — Comme Renan hélas, comme Chateaubriand, en désespoir...".

46. The basis of the constant comparison between life in the colonies and the life he had known at the front seems to be that to Bardamu and to others the two styles of life have much in common. "C'était l'homme du 'corocoro' qui nous régalait. Il nous fit même marcher son phonographe.

On trouvait de tout dans sa boutique. Ça me rappelait les convois de la guerre." *Oeuvres*, I, 103; "En paix comme à la guerre, je n'étais point disposé du tout aux futilités." *Ibid.*, I, 107; "Je dus lui sembler tout à fait navré au copain car il m'interpella assez brusquement pour me faire sortir de mes réflexions. 'allez donc, vous serez moins mal encore ici qu'à la guerre! Ici, aprés tout, on peut se débrouiller!'" *Ibid.*, I, 121. An example of the link between the war and the United States is furnished perhaps most obviously by Lola: "En somnolant à ses côtés, les temps passés me revinrent en mémoire, ces temps où Lola m'avait quitté dans Paris de la guerre. ..." *Ibid.*, I, 159; Finally, sometimes Céline overlaps all three places, the front, Africa, and America, as for instance when Bardamu asks for directions in the streets of Detroit: "Ils m'ont parlé les passants comme le sergent m'avait parlé dans la forêt. 'Voilà qu'ils m'ont dit. Vous pouvez pas vous tromper, c'est juste en face de vous." *Ibid.*, I, 164.

47. Céline himself admitted to Milton Hindus in a letter of May 29, 1947, that the play was a "flop." "Quant à *L'Eglise* elle fut en effet représentée à Lyon par des amateurs — Ce fut un four à hurler [flop] total — Il faudrait un prodigieux metteur en scène pour mettre cela debout, vivant, pimpant, snappy à l'américaine — Je n'ai pas le don du théâtre — du dialogue seulement — La pièce est ratée — Je n'aime pas les échecs — Certes il me plairait bien de la faire jouer aux USA mais qui s'en chargerait? Il faudrait l'abréger d'abord — Elle est trop longue. ..." *L'Herne*, V (1965), 76.

48. In addition to reviews of this revival, cited in Chapter 1, note 21, above, see also *Oeuvres*, I, 377 - 492, for the text of *L'Eglise*. According to Jean-A. Ducourneau, in his notes to this edition of the play, its presentation in Lyons on December 4, 1936, at the Théâtre des Célestins lasted five hours (I, 759).

49. Ostrowsky, *Céline and His Vision*, p. 6.

50. Bettina L. Knapp, *Céline: Man of Hate* (University, Alabama, 1974), p. 55.

51. Thiher, *The Novel As Delirium*, p. 121.

52. This is our translation of the following passage: "Voilà! J'aime mieux les rapports avec ceux qui sont malades. Ceux qui sont bien portants, sont si méchants, si bêtes; ils veulent avoir l'air si malins, aussitôt qu'ils tiennent debout, que tout rapport avec eux est presque aussitôt malheureux! Quand ils sont couchés et qu'ils souffrent, ils vous foutent la paix. Vous comprenez?" *Oeuvres*, I, 452.

53. Here are Céline's stage directions for Judenzweck's arrival on stage: "Pendant que tout ce brouhaha a lieu sur la scène, un petit homme, habillé en juif polonais, long cache-poussière noir, petite casquette, lunettes épaisses, nez extrêmement crochu, parapluie, guêtres, se glisse, prudent, très prudent, venant de la salle, le long des loges. Il monte vers la scène, furtif et un peu caché. Il fait signe, avant de monter, à Miss Broum, qui répond à son signe. ..." *Oeuvres*, I, 439.

54. "Ce qui est plus triste que tout, écoutez-moi, c'est de mourir. (Il y a même que ça de triste dans la vie. Et d'ailleurs, s'il y avait pas ça, on n'aimerait pas, comme vous dites;) l'amour, c'est de la peur de mourir." *Oeuvres*, I, 488.

Chapter Three

1. *Mort à crédit* has been well translated by Ralph Manheim, *Death on the Installment Plan* (New York: 1966), p. 19. "Mon tourment à moi, c'est le sommeil. Si j'avais bien dormi toujours j'aurais jamais écrit une ligne..." *Oeuvres*, II, 8.

2. *Death*, p. 22. "... j'avais presque de quoi en moi me payer la mort! ... J'étais un rentier d'Esthétique. J'en avais mangé de la fesse et de la merveilleuse ... je dois le confesser de la vraie lumière. J'avais bouffé de l'infini." *Oeuvres*, II, 10.

3. Critics are sometimes tempted to call *Voyage* a Naturalistic novel. Despite Céline's often quoted speech *Hommage à Zola*, delivered at Médan on October 10, 1933, to the circle of "Amis d'Emile Zola" at the request of Lucien Descaves, the critic who had supported *Voyage* for the Goncourt Prize, the adjective still seems inappropriate. In fact, Céline had little or no sympathy with Zola's work and said as much in this speech. In a letter written to Evelyne Pollet just a few weeks before this talk, he had written: "Justes Cieux je n'aime pas Zola" (*Oeuvres*, II, 727). The text of this address, with good background notes, can be found in *Oeuvres*, II, 501-507.

4. Pierre Hahn, "Sur L.-F. Céline," *Marginales*, nos. 80 - 81 november - décembre 1961) 71 - 74, argues that Céline should really be called a "pointilliste" for his use of popular language, slangy metaphors, syncopated syntax, and, of course, the three little dots.

5. Thiher, *The Novel As Delirium*, p. 49.

6. *Death*, p. 55. "Elle a fait tout pour que je vive, c'est naître qu'il aurait pas fallu." *Oeuvres*, II, 35.

7. *Death*, p. 76. "Aussitôt qu'elle était partie, ça manquait jamais, je bondissais aux gogs, au troisiéme, me taper un violent rassis. Je redescendais tout cerné." *Oeuvres*, II, 52.

8. This scene, found on pages 179 - 87 of the Manheim translation, was the subject of curious speculation by French reviewers of *Mort* when it first appeared. This is so because Céline and his publisher Denoël agreed to delete a number of paragraphs from the novel in advance of publication, since they feared that inclusion of these paragraphs might provoke a legal problem with potential censors. Thus, the absence of this whole passage was indicated by the presence of gaping white spaces on the printed page. The modern texts found in the Pléiade and Balland editions, as well as in the Manheim translation, are integral.

9. *Death*, p. 241. "Pour Nora, l'idiot, il était un tintouin affreux, elle aurait pu être épuisée à la fin des après-midi ... Rien qu'à le moucher, le faire pisser, le retenir à chaque instant de passer sous les voitures, d'avaler des trucs au hasard, de tout déglutir, c'était une corvée ignoble ..." *Oeuvres*, II, 178.

10. *Journey*, p. 425. "... pourriture en suspens ..." *Oeuvres*, I, 310.

11. Hindus, p. 27. "Resensibiliser la langue, qu'elle palpite plus qu'elle ne raisonne." *L'Herne*, V (1965), 75.

12. Hindus, p. 26. "Encore est-ce un truc pour faire passer le langage parlé en écrit — le truc c'est moi qui l'ai trouvé personne autre ... Faire passer le langage parlé en littérature — ce n'est pas la sténographie — Il faut imprimer aux phrases, aux périodes une certaine déformation un artifice tel que lorsque vous lisez le livre il semble que l'on vous parle à l'oreille — Cela s'obtient par une transposition de chaque mot qui n'est jamais tout à fait celui qu'on attend une menue surprise. Il se passe ce qui aurait lieu pour un bâton plongé dans l'eau pour qu'il vous apparaisse droit il faut avant de le plonger dans l'eau que vous le cassiez légèrement si j'ose dire que vous le tordiez, préalablement. Un bâton correctement droit au contraire plongé dans l'eau apparaît tordu au regard. De même du langage — le dialogue le plus sténographié, semble sur la page plat, compliqué et lourd ..." *L'Herne* V (1965), 73.

13. Hindus, p. 26. "Pour rendre sur la page l'effet de la vie parlée spontanée il faut tordre la langue en tout rythme, cadence, mots et ç'est une sorte de poésie qui donne le meilleur sortilège — *l'impression, l'envoûtement, le dynamisme* —et puis il faut aussi choisir son sujet — Tout n'est pas *transposable* — Il faut des sujets 'à vifs' — d'où les terribles risques — pour lire tous les secrets." *L'Herne*, V (1965), 73. (The reader should note that Hindus mistranslates the last sentence.)

14. Montourcy, pp. 9 - 10; and Brochard, pp. 13 - 17.

15. Rebatet, pp. 43 - 45.

16. *Oeuvres*, II, 713.

17. *Ibid*.

18. One might recall here his remark in a letter to Hindus to the effect that: "... la vérité ne me suffit plus — Il me faut une transposition de tout ..." *L'Herne*, V (1965), 84.

19. Hindus, p. 32. "Ce qui ne chante pas n'existe pas pour l'âme — merde pour la réalité. Je veux mourir en musique pas en raison ni en prose. Les hommes ne méritent pas que l'on se restreigne de délirer pour eux." *L'Herne*, V (1965), 84.

20. Michel Beaujour, "La Quête du délire," *L'Herne*, III (1963), 283. "Ainsi donc le délire est ambivalent, à la fois ce qui permet de vivre, malgré tout, et composante du malheur de l'Homme, puisque le monde est une somme de délires qui se heurtent. ... C'est pourquoi les asiles d'aliénés jouent un tel rôle dans le *Voyage*: lieux bénis où les vrais fous entre eux,

protégés du monde agité de délires plus meurtriers, peuvent coïncider pleinement avec leurs divagations. La véritable catastrophe, qui menace toujours, c'est la retombée du délire, la perte de l'illusion globable."

21. Léon Daudet, *Le Rêve éveillé* (Paris: Grasset, 1926).

22. *Ibid.*, p. 12. "Le rêve éveillé est, chez l'homme, la matière de l'imagination, le réservoir où puise constamment (et, à l'état normal, librement) l'imagination."

23. Colin W. Nettelbeck, "Journey to the End of Art: The Evolution of the Novels of Louis-Ferdinand Céline," *PMLA*, LXXXVII (1972), 83 - 84.

24. "Hommage à Zola," *L'Herne*, III (1963), 169 - 70.

25. *Bagatelles pour un massacre* (Paris: Denoël, 1938), p. 218. "Pour mon petit personnel je dois beaucoup à Barbusse, à Daudet du *Rêve éveillé*." It was in Barbusse's war novel *Le Feu* (1916) that Céline found the reproduction of everyday speech. Where Barbusse reproduced what he had heard, transforming orthography when necessary to transmit accent and intonation, Céline transposed the very essence of spoken language in his own prose.

26. Thiher, *The Novel As Delirium*, p. 53.

27. *Ibid.*, p. 53.

28. Nettelbeck, p. 82.

29. Hindus, p. 27. "Je suis celte avant tout *révasseur bardique* ..." *L'Herne*, V (1965), 76.

30. Hindus, p. 27. "Je peux raconter des légendes comme on pisse, avec une facilité qui me dégoûte, des scénarios, des ballets tant qu'on veut, en bavardant c'est vraiment là mon don — je l'ai plié au réalisme par esprit de haine de la méchanceté des hommes — par esprit de combat — mais en réalité ma musique c'est la légende et je ne les sors pas des bibliothèques ou du folklore chinois comme tous les néo-bardes mais absolument de mon cru, absolument de moi seul ..." *L'Herne*, V (1965), 76.

31. *Oeuvres*, II, 737. "Un tel pari contre l'humanité ne se soutient pendant sept cents pages qu'à coups d'artifices."

32. Rennes: Imprimerie Francis Simon, 1924.

33. In 1937 it was added by Denoël to the text of *Mea Culpa* and published under the latter title. The English translation of both works by Robert Allerton Parker was published almost immediately and we quote from it: *Mea Culpa and The Life and Work of Semmelweis* (Boston: Little, Brown and Co., 1937).

34. Published in volume I of the Balland edition of the *Oeuvres*, it occupies pp. 577 - 621. By contrast, *Voyage* occupies almost four hundred pages in the same volume.

35. *Semmelweis*, p. 45. "Du coup, vingt races se précipitèrent dans un affreux délire. ... se ruèrent à la conquête d'un Idéal." *Oeuvres*, I, 582.

36. *Semmelweis*, p. 45. "... Napoléon prit l'Europe et, bon gré mal gré, la garda quinze ans." *Oeuvres*, I, 582.

37. *Semmelweis*, p. 39. 'Il démontre le danger de vouloir trop de bien aux hommes. C'est une vieille leçon toujours jeune." *Oeuvres*, I, 579.

38. *Semmelweis*, p. 96. "Si on meurt moins chez Bartch ..... c'est que chez lui le toucher est exclusivement pratiqué par des élèves sages-femmes alors que chez Klin les étudiants procèdent à la même manoeuvre chez les femmes enceintes sans aucune douceur et provoquent par leur brutalité une inflammation fatale." *Oeuvres*, I, 597.

39. *Semmelweis*, p. 99. "Dans son ardeur à la recherche, il s'est retranché de la vie courante, il l'ignore, il n'existe plus que passionnellement ..." *Oeuvres*, I, 598.

40. *Semmelweis*, p. 149. "'J'ai d'ailleurs longuement pensé à ces mortalités que vous observiez jadis chez Klin et je vais, moi, vous en donner, je crois, la raison. Klin ne purgeait pas méthodiquement ses accoucnées, ici ...'" *Oeuvres*, I, 613.

41. *Die Aetiologie des Begriff und die Prophylaxis des Kindbettfiebers* (Pest: 1861).

42. *Semmelweis*, p. 152. "Assassins! je les appelle tous ceux qui s'élèvent contre les règles que j'ai prescrites pour éviter la fièvre puerpérale." *Oeuvres*, I, 614.

43. *Semmelweis*, p. 159. "Arneth était raisonnable, Semmelweis ne l'était plus. Estimer, prévoir, attendre surtout semblaient d'impossibles tyrannies à son espirt en déroute." *Oeuvres*, I, 616.

44. *Semmelweis*, pp. 167 - 69; *Oeuvres*, I, 619.

Vers deux heures, on le vit dévaler à travers les rues, poursuivi par la meute de ses ennemis fictifs. C'est en hurlant, débraillé, qu'il parvint de la sorte jusqu'aux amphithéâtres d'anatomie de la Faculté. Un cadavre était là, sur le marbre, au milieu du cours, pour une démonstration. Semmelweis s'emparant d'un scalpel, franchit le cercle des élèves, bousculant plusieurs chaises, s'approche du marbre, incise la peau du cadavre et taille dans les tissus putrides, avant qu'on ait pu l'empêcher, au hasard de ses impulsions, détachant les muscles par lambeaux qu'il projette au loin. Il accompagne ses manoeuvres d'exclamations et de phrases sans suite... .
Les étudiants l'ont reconnu, mais son attitude est si menaçante que personne n'ose l'interrompre ... Il ne sait plus ... Il reprend son scalpel et fouille avec ses doigts en même temps qu'avec la lame une cavité cadavérique suintante d'humeurs. Par un geste plus saccadé que les autres il se coupe profondément.
Sa blessure saigne. Il crie. Il menace. On le désarme. On l'entoure. Mais il est trop tard ...
Comme Kolletchka naguère, il vient de s'infecter mortellement.

45. *Semmelweis*, p. 172. "... une forme délirante ..." *Oeuvres*, I, 620.

46. *Semmelweis*, p. 173. "... il entra dans une sorte de verbiage incessant, dans une réminiscence interminable, au cours de laquelle sa tête brisée parut se vider en longues phrases mortes." *Oeuvres*, I, 620.

47. *Semmelweis*, p. 173. "Ce n'était plus cette infernale reconstitution

de sa vie sur un plan de délire dont il avait été à Budapest l'acteur tyrannisé aux premiers temps de sa folie." *Oeuvres*, I, 620.

48. *Semmelweis*, p. 118. "L'homme est un être sentimental. Point de grandes créations hors du sentiment, et l'enthousiasme vite s'épuise chez la plupart d'entre eux à mesure qu'ils s'éloignent de leur rêve." *Oeuvres*, I, 603.

49. *Semmelweis*, p. 62. "Dans l'Histoire des temps la vie n'est qu'une ivresse, la Vérité c'est la Mort." *Oeuvres*, I, 587.

50. *Semmelweis*, p. 62. "Enfin, Semmelweis puisait son existence à des sources trop généreuses pour être bien compris par les autres hommes. Il était de ceux, trop rares, qui peuvent aimer la vie dans ce qu'elle a de plus simple et de plus beau: vivre." *Oeuvres*, I, 587.

51. *Oeuvres* II, 447 - 99; 725 - 27. Originally published in the *Cahiers de la Pléiade* under the title "Le Casse-Pipe" (an editorial error), this fragment contained but one chapter. The second chapter was published as an appendix to Poulet's *Entretiens familiers avec L.-F. Céline*, pp. 103 - 13. Two other fragments were later published in *L'Herne*, III (1963), 167 - 68. The reader is alerted that the Gallimard volume entitled *Casse-Pipe*, published in 1952 and reissued in 1970, contains only chapter one.

52. A note in *L'Herne* III (1963), 167, unsigned, tells us: "Commencé en 1936, *Casse-Pipe* devait être la suite de *Mort à crédit*. Le manuscrit disparut à la Libération, sans doute dans une poubelle, comme la bibliothèque et les papiers de Céline. ..."

Chapter Four

1. In addition to Milton Hindus's *The Crippled Giant* (New York, 1950); see also his "Céline: A Reappraisal," *Southern Review*, I (1965), 76 - 93, and "The Recent Revival of Céline: A Consideration," *Mosaic,* VI (1973), 57 - 66.

Other critics worth reading on the question are Nigel Dennis, "I Bite Everywhere," *The New York Review of Books*, February 10, 1972, pp. 3 - 6; Colin W. Nettelbeck, "The Antisemite and the Artist: Céline's Pamphlets and *Guignol's Band*," *Australian Journal of French Studies*, IX (1972), 181 - 89; and George Steiner, "Cry Havoc," *The New Yorker*, January 20, 1968, pp. 106 - 15.

2. In fact several of them did not. See our article "Eugène Dabit: A French Working Class Novelist," *Research Studies*, XXXIX (1973), 217 - 33.

3. Gide, *Retour de l'U.R.S.S.* (1936); and Pierre Herbart, *En U.R.S.S.* (1937).

4. Poulet, p. 6.

5. *Mea Culpa* was originally published by Denoël and Steele in 1937. Later, when Céline signed a contract with Gallimard, the latter did not buy

the rights to this work. It has been reprinted in *Oeuvres* III, 335 - 47. As mentioned above, Céline's doctoral thesis was appended to it and both works were translated and published in one volume in English under the title *Mea Culpa* (Boston: Little Brown and Co., 1937). We quote from this edition.

6. *Mea Culpa*, p. 9. "Se faire voir aux côtés du peuple, par les temps qui courent, c'est prendre une 'assurance-nougat.' Pourvu qu'on se sente un peu juif ça devient une 'assurance-vie.' Tout cela est fort compréhensible." *Oeuvres*, III, 339.

7. *Mea Culpa*, p. 13. "Le peuple est Roi! ... Le Roi la saute! Il a tout! Il manque de chemise!" *Oeuvres*, III, 340.

8. *Mea Culpa*, pp. 33 - 34. "Ils essayent de farcir l'étron, de la faire passer au caramel." *Oeuvres*, III, 346.

9. *Mea Culpa*, p. 35. "Avec les juifs, sans les juifs. Tout ça n'a pas d'importance! ..." *Oeuvres*, III, 346.

10. *Ecole des cadavres* was republished by Denoël in 1943. The five volume *Oeuvres* of Céline cannot be called complete mainly because it does not contain these three pamphlets. Céline's widow, in asking that they not be reprinted, is said to be carrying out Céline's wish in this matter.

11. Steiner, p. 110.

12. *Ibid.*, p. 106.

13. André Gide, "Eugène Dabit," *La Nouvelle Revue Française,* XLVII (1936), 581 - 90.

14. "Je n'adhère qu'à moi-même, autant que possible ..." p. 45. We quote here from *Bagatelles pour un massacre* (Paris, 1937). The translations are our own.

15. "Moi, j'ai encore la mentalité d'un ouvrier d'avant-guerre." *Ibid.*, p.46.

16. See Chapter 1, note 22.

17. These two key expressions are used quite frequently in *Bagatelles.*

18. Albert Chesneau, *Essai de psychocritique de Louis-Ferdinand Céline* (Paris, 1971).

19. *Ibid.*, p. 40 "Les *Ballets* ne sont donc pas que des fantaisies poétiques, mais aussi de très transparentes et très sérieuses allégories qui appellent au retour aux sources, exigent l'éviction des Etrangers de race impure et prêchent contre eux une nouvelle croisade." These three ballets, joined to two others, *Scandale aux abysses* (*Scandal in the Depths*) (Paris: Chambriand, 1950) and *Foudres et flèches* (*Sparks and Arrows*), (Paris: Charles de Jonquières, 1949), were republished in *Ballets sans musique, sans personne, sans rien* (Paris, 1959). These last two works take Greco-Roman mythological characters as their point of departure.

20. Rebatet, p. 49.

21. *Ecole des cadavres* (Paris, 1938), p. 62. "Personnellement, je trouve Hitler, Franco, Mussolini fabuleusement débonnaires, admirablement

magnanimes, infiniment trop à mon sens, pacifistes bêlants pour tour dire, à 250 Prix Nobel, hors concours, par acclamations!"

22. *Ibid.,* p. 84. "Tous les Aryens devraient avoir lu Drummont. Plus actuels: De Vries, De Poncins, Sombart, Stanley Chamberlain; plus prés: Montandon, Darquier de Pellepoix, Boissel, H.-R. Petit, Dasté, H. Coston, des Essards, Alex, Santo, etc. ... Vous trouverez une bibliographie française très achalandée au Centre Documentaire, 10 rue d'Argenteuil, au Rassemblement anti-Juif, 12 rue Laugier."

23. *Ibid.,* p. 98 - 99. "S'il avait envie de "redresser," comme il annonçait, Daladier, il avait pas besoin pour ça de se répandre en 500 décrets. Trois suffisaient, très largement. Des bons, des effectifs: (1) L'expulsion de tous les Juifs. (2) Interdiction, fermeture de toutes les Loges et Sociétés Secrètes. (3) Travaux forcés à perpétuité pour toutes les personnes pas satisfaites, dures d'oreilles, etc. ..."

24. René Heron de Villefosse, "Prophéties et litanies de Céline," *L'Herne,* III (1963), 34.

25. Ostrowsky, *Céline and His Vision,* pp. 97 - 99. The French right had been anti-German all through the early thirties, usually calling for stern measures to be taken against the illegal rearming of Germany. But by 1938, when it became obvious that France could no longer hope to win a war against Germany, the right sought to appease Hitler. But Céline, in calling for a Franco-German alliance, went further than even the average French Fascist of the day was willing to go.

26. Geoffroy, p. 12. We know that Céline read Nietzsche while convalescing in London during the war.

27. Pol Vandromme, *Louis-Ferdinand Céline* (Paris, 1963). Vandromme is the most articulate spokesman for those critics who do not see Céline as an anti-Semite. On the contrary, they attribute to his use of the word "Jew" a symbolic value synonymous with "elite" and *"Bourgeoisie."* Among Vandromme's other articles on Céline are "Louis-Ferdinand Céline," *Revue Générale Belge,* XVII (1961), 23-31; and "L'Esprit des pamphlets," *L'Herne,* III (1963), 272 - 76.

28. Vandromme, *Céline,* pp. 18 - 24.

29. *Les Beaux draps* (Paris, 1941), p. 20. "le frère suçon du bourgeois."

30. *Ibid.,* p. 30. "Personne veut du sacrifice. Tout le monde veut du bénéfice. Nougat 100 pour 100."

31. *Ibid.,* p. 156. "C'est comme pour devenir pro-allemand, j'attends pas que la Commandatur pavoise au Crillon."

32. Rebatet, p. 46. "Ils ont paumé, et nous avec. Une armée qui n'apporte pas une révolution avec, dans les guerres comme celle-ci, elle est cuite. Tordus, les Frizous."

33. *Draps,* p. 144. "Le Juif a peur seulement que d'une chose: du Communisme sans les Juifs."

34. *Ibid.,* p. 115. "... ça vous écoeure tous les journaux dits

farouchement antisémites. Qu'est-ce qu'ils cherchent au fond? On se demande. Qu'est-ce qu'ils veulent? la place des youpins? carrer là-dedans leurs chères personnes? C'est mince comme programme.''

35. *Ibid.*, p. 183. "L'Elite n'est-ce pas c'est Exemple ou alors c'est rien du tout.''

36. Chesneau, pp. 89 - 93.

37. See Chapter 1, note 22.

38. Pierre de Boisdeffre, "Sur la postérité de Céline,'' *L'Herne*, V (1965), 221.

39. André Gide, "Les Juifs, Céline et Maritain,'' *La Nouvelle Revue Française* (avril 1938), 630 - 34; and Sartre, p. 462.

40. McCarthy, pp. 139 - 69.

41. *Rigadoon*, translated by Ralph Manheim, (New York; 1974), p. 260. "Il va de soi! détail! ... l'important le sang! ... le sang seul est sérieux!'' *Oeuvres*, V, 500.

42. *Rigadoon*, p. 190. "... je ne veux rien faire revivre du tout! ... l'Europe est morte à Stalingrad ... le Diable a son âme! qu'il la garde! ...'' *Oeuvres*, V, 345.

43. *Rigadoon*, p. 107. "Non! biologiste j'ai dit, c'est tout! ...seule la biologie existe, le reste est blabla! ... tout le reste! ... je maintiens, au 'Bal des Gamètes' la grande ronde du monde, les noirs, les jaunes gagnent toujours! ... les blancs sont toujours perdants ...'' *Oeuvres*, V, 402.

Chapter Five

1. *Le Pont de Londres* (Paris, 1962). This novel has not been translated into English. The first half of the novel was published under the title of *Guignol's Band* (Paris, 1944).

2. Since the first half of *Guignol's Band* has been well translated and published under the same English title by B. Frechtman and J. T. Nile (New York, 1954), we quote from it here, p. 3. "Je les trouve en projet, pas écrits, mort-nés, ni faits ni à faire, la vie qui manque ...'' *Oeuvres*, II, 518.

3. *Guignol*, p. 4. "Le Jazz a renversé la valse, l'Impressionisme a tué le 'faux jour,' vous écrirez 'télégraphique' ou vous écrirez plus du tout.'' *Oeuvres*, II, 519.

4. *Guignol*, p.1. "Et s'ils l'apprennent au bachot, dans deux cents ans et les Chinois? Qu'est ce que vous direz?'' *Oeuvres*, II, 517.

5. *Guignol*, p. 33. "... anges riants ...'' *Oeuvres*, II, 536.

6. *Guignol*, p. 149. "... il se disait des choses à lui-même comme ça en plutôt yiddish, fallait qu'on le comprenne à mi-mots ...'' *Oeuvres*, II, 611.

7. See Chapter 4, note 19.

8. *Pont de Londres* is included in the Balland edition of the *Oeuvres*. "... je me trouvais rêveur éveillé ...,'' III, 278. See also our discussion in Chapter Three of Céline's use of delirium scenes.

9. See Allen Thiher, "The Yet to Be Salvaged Céline: *Guignol's Band*," *Modern Fiction Studies*, SVI (1970), 67 - 75, who sees this work as a "delirious romance where youth acts out a parody of its obsessions" (p. 75); and Nettelbeck, "The Antisemite and the Artist," in which the novel is considered to be a step in Céline's process of self-regeneration. The murder of Van Claben is seen as an anti-Semitic act, but then the subsequent murder of Mille-Pattes is taken as a metaphor for the rejection of the decadent civilization that had tolerated the first murder. Thus, free of decadence, Ferdinand is finally able to believe in an ideal incarnated in Sosthène. To Nettelbeck, the latter "is an archetype of the ancient spiritual and mythological values of which Céline speaks so nostalgically in the pamphlets" (p. 186). We find that this interpretation overstates its case somewhat.

10. Neither *Féerie pour une autre fois I* (Paris, 1952) nor *Normance: Féerie pour une autre fois II* (Paris, 1954) has been translated into English.

11. "Confusion des lieux, des temps! Merde! C'est la féerie vous comprenez ..." *Oeuvres*, III, 431. The translation is ours.

12. "Les Ricains ont un retard honteux! Ils ont deux siècles de retard, nigauds! bafouilleurs menteurs!" *Oeuvres*, III, 557.

13. "Je récapitule ... je condense ... c'est le style 'Digest' ... les gens ont que le temps de lire trente pages ... il paraît! au plus! ... c'est l'exigence! ils déconnent seize heures sur vingt-quatre, ils dorment, ils coïtent le reste, comment auraient-ils le temps de lire cent pages? et de faire caca, j'oublie." *Oeuvres*, III, 555.

14. *North*, translated by Ralph Manheim (New York, 1971), pp. 346 - 47. "... le petit succès de mon existence c'est d'avoir tout de même réussi ce tour de force qu'ils se trouvent tous d'accord, un instant, droite, gauche, centre, sacristies, loges, cellules, charniers, le comte de Paris, Joéphine, ma tante Odile, Kroukroubezoff, l'abbé Tirelire, que je suis le plus grand ordure vivant!" *Oeuvres*, V, 260.

15. Albert Paraz, "Extraits de lettres d'Albert Paraz à Pierre Marcat sur Céline," *L'Herne*, V (1965), 297. "Pour *Normance*, vous avez eu tort de vouloir le lire comme un roman. C'est une apocalypse. Prenez la Bible et lisez-la, vous verrez qu'on ne peut pas la lire en une fois. Il faut déguster *Normance* page par page. Et croyez-moi, Céline pouvait écrire une suite de *Guignol's Band*, si ça lui avait plu. Il a cherché un autre mode d'expression, c'est son droit d'artiste."

16. "L'émotion dans le langage écrit! ... le langage écrit était à sec, c'est moi qu'ai redonné l'émotion au langage écrit! ... comme je vous le dis! ... c'est pas qu'un petit turbin je vous jure! ..." *Oeuvres*, III, 357.

17. "... je vous livre la vérité tout pure ... profitez de ce que je vous dis! ... soyez prévenu: je laisse rien au cinéma! je lui ai embarqué ses effets! ... toute sa rastaquouérie-mélo! ... tout son simili-sensible! ... tous ses effets! décanté, épuré, tout ça! ..." *Oeuvres*, III, 395.

18. "... mon métro à 'traverses trois points' emporte tout! ... mon métro magique! ... délateurs, beautés suspectes, quais brumeux, autos, petits chiens, immeubles tout neufs, chalets romantiques ..." *Oeuvres*, III, 395.

19. "La loi du genre. pas de lyrisme sans 'je', Colonel! Notez, je vous prie, Colonel! ... la Loi du lyrisme!" *Oeuvres*, III, 374.

20. "L'argot a son rôle, oui! ... certes! ... l'histoire de tous les piments! ... y en a pas? ... votre brouet est con! ... y en a trop? ... encore plus con! ... il y faut un tact! ..." *Oeuvres*, III, 377.

21. "Pas simplement à son oreille! ... non! ... dans l'intimité de ses nerfs! en plein dans son système nerveux! dans sa propre tête! *Oeuvres*, III, 397.

22. *Oeuvres*, III, 398.

23. "... ma petite découverte bouleverse pas seulement le roman! ... le cinéma capote de même! parfaitement! elle fout en l'air le cinéma! oui! lui-même! il existera plus! *Oeuvres*, III, 382.

24. "Il n'y a qu'une seule langue, Colonel, en ce monde paracafouilleux! une seule langue valable! respectable! la langue impériale de ce monde: la nôtre! ... charabias, les autres, vous m'entendez? ..." *Oeuvres*, III, 391.

Chapter Six

1. See Chapter 1, note 27.

2. In addition to *Casse-Pipe*, of which we now possess several fragments, he also refers to a text called *Volonté du Roi Krogold* (*Will of King Krogold*), of which we have no trace. We recall that the "Legend of King Krogold" is a recurring theme in the first part of *Mort à crédit*.

3. Roger Vailland, "Nous n'épargnerons pas Céline," *La Tribune des Nations*, 1 (13 janvier 1950), 5; Claude Dubois, "Vailland contre Céline," *La Quinzaine Littéraire*, 1-15 avril 1969, pp. 22 - 23. See also, Champfleury, *L'Herne*, III, 60 - 66.

4. Thiher, "Céline and Sartre," *Philological Quarterly*; L (1971), pp. 292 - 305.

5. "j'ai attrapé la 'fusion' au Cameroon 1917! ... la fièvre monte encore! ... le moment des idées! ..." *Oeuvres*, IV, 328.

6. We quote here from the fine translation by Ralph Manheim, *Castle to Castle* (New York, 1968), p. 113. "Oh, que j'étais bien décidé à plus rien écrire ... j'ai toujours trouvé indécent, rien que le mot: écrire! ... prétentiard, narcisse, 'm'as-tu lu' ... c'est donc bien la raison de la gêne ... la seule! ..." *Oeuvres*, IV, 329.

7. *Castle*, p. 111. "... mémorialiste ..." *Oeuvres*, IV, 329.

8. *Castle*, p. 205. "... mais je vous parle en clinicien, embryologiste et raciste ... que ce mariage ... ait donné une si belle enfant ..." *Oeuvres*, IV, 389.

9. *Castle*, p. 61. "c'est le *Voyage* qui m'a fait tout le tort ... mes pires

haineux acharnés sont venus du *Voyage* ... Personne m'a pardonné le *Voyage* ... depuis le *Voyage* mon compte est bon! ..." *Oeuvres*, IV, 296.

10. *Castle*, p. 38. "... je trouve pas le *Voyage* tellement drôle ... Altman non plus le trouvait pas drôle ... ni Daudet ..." *Oeuvres*, IV, 284.

11. *Castle*, p. 321. "... du coup je les affranchis aussi, la Délégation, que c'est moi l'auteur du premier roman communiste qu'a jamais été écrit ... qu'ils en écriront jamais d'autres! jamais! ... qu'ils ont pas la tripe! ..." *Oeuvres*, IV, 468.

12. *North*, p. 4. "... chroniqueur ..." *Oeuvres*, V, 14.

13. *North*, p. 281. "Oh, vous savez ... vos livres ... depuis le *Voyage* ... Vous ne pouvez plus attendre grand-chose ..." *Oeuvres*, V, 285.

14. *North*, p. 143, "j'ai été élevé je peux dire, toute mon enfance et la jeunesse, dans le labeur et les nouilles à l'eau ..." *Oeuvres*, V, 115.

15. *North*, p. 106, "... anarchiste suis, été, demeure, et me fous bien des opinions! ... *Oeuvres*, V, 84.

16. *North*, p. 124, "... le vrai rideau de fer c'est entre les riches et les miteux ..." *Oeuvres*, V, 102.

17. *North*, p. 236 "je vois moi avec 'Les Beaux draps' qu'étaient qu'une chronique de l'époque ce que j'ai entendu!" *Oeuvres*, V, 185.

18. *Rigadoon*, p. 215 "même mon idée depuis toujours, preuve que tous les droits de mes belles oeuvres, à peu près six millions de francs étaient là-haut ... pas au petit bonheur, en coffre et en banque ... je peux le dire à présent *Landsman Bank* ... *Peter Bang Wej* ..." *Oeuvres*, V, 470.

19. *Rigadoon*, p. 257, "les dettes, si vous êtes ministre, ne comptent pas ... si vous êtes d'une Académie on comprendra vos faiblesses ... mais là moi vous vous rendez compte, j'aurais beau parler du *Voyage*, que c'est une date, que tout ce qui fut écrit depuis n'est que 'pénibles imitations, galimatias tièdes' ... comment on ma'enverra foutre! ... *Oeuvres*, V, 498.

20. *Rigadoon*, p. 260. "Il va de soi! détail! ... l'important le sang! ... le sang seul est sérieux!" *Oeuvres*, V, 500.

21. *Rigadoon*, p. 107. "Parasitologiste je suis! grogneugneu! diplômé! n'oubliez pas!" *Oeuvres*, V, 402.

22. *Rigadoon*, p. 107. "Non! biologiste j'ai dit, c'est tout! ... seul la biologie existe, le reste, est blabla! ... tout le reste! ... je maintiens, au 'Bal des Gamètes' la grande ronde du monde, les noirs, les jaunes gagnent toujours! ... les blancs sont toujours perdants ..." *Oeuvres*, V, 402.

23. *Rigadoon*, p. 19. "... je ne veux rien faire revivre du tout! ... l'Europe est morte à Stalingrad ... le Diable a son âme! qu'il la garde! ... *Oeuvres*, V, 345.

Selected Bibliography

PRIMARY SOURCES

(Note: French books are published in Paris unless otherwise stated.)

With the exception of the three pamphlets, *Bagatelles, Ecole,* and *Les Beaux draps,* listed below, all other texts are included in the five volume *Oeuvres de Louis-Ferdinand Céline,* Balland, 1966-69, from which we have quoted whenever possible in this volume.

A l'agité du bocal. P. Lanauve de Tartas, 1948. Reprinted in *L'Herne,* V (1965), 22-27.

Bagatelles pour un massacre. Denoël, 1937. Reprinted with photographs in 1943.

Ballets sans musique, sans personne, sans rien. Gallimard, 1957. (This volume contains the five ballets *Scandale aux abysses, La Naissance d'une fée, Voyou Paul brave Virginie, Van Bagaden,* and *Foudres et fléches.*)

Les Beaux draps. Les Nouvelles Editions, 1941.

Casse-Pipe. Fragment appended to R. Poulet's *Entretiens familiers avec L.-F. Céline.* Plon, 1958, 1971, pp. 103-13. Another fragment in *L'Herne,* III (1963), 167-68. See also: *Casse-Pipe,* Gallimard, 1952, 1970.

D'un château l'autre. Gallimard, 1957. Translated by Ralph Manheim as *Castle to Castle.* New York, Delacorte, 1968. Pléiade Edition, 1976.

L'Ecole des cadavres. Denoël, 1938. Reprinted with preface in 1942.

L'Eglise, comédie en cinq actes. Denoël et Steele, 1933.

Entretiens avec le professeur Y... Gallimard, 1955.

Féerie pour une autre fois I. Gallimard, 1952.

Guignol's Band I. Denoel, 1944, and Gallimard, 1952. Translated by Bernard Frechtman and Jack T. Nile as *Guignol's Band.* New York, New Directions, 1954.

Mea Culpa. (Followed by *La Vie et l'oeuvre de Semmelweis.*) Denoël et Steele, 1937. Translated and introduced by Robert Allerton Parker as *Mea Culpa and The Life and Work of Semmelweis.* Boston: Little, Brown, 1937.

Mort à crédit. Denoël et Steele, 1936, and Gallimard, 1962 (Pléiade
  Edition). Translated by Ralph Manheim as *Death on the Installment
  Plan.* New York, New Directions, 1966. Originally translated by John
  H. P. Marks under the same title. Boston: Little, Brown, 1938.
Nord. Gallimard, 1960. Translated by Ralph Manheim as *North.* New
  York, Delacorte, 1971. Pléiade Edition, 1976.
Normance: Féerie pour une autre fois II. Gallimard, 1954.
Le Pont de Londres: Guignol's Band II. Gallimard, 1964.
La Quinine en thérapeutique. Doin, 1925.
Rigodon. Gallimard, 1969. Translated by Ralph Manehim as *Rigadoon.*
  New York, Delacorte, 1974. Pléiade Edition, 1976.
La Vie et l'oeuvre de Philippe-Ignace Semmelweis. Rennes: Francis Simon,
  1924, and Gallimard, 1952.
Voyage au bout de la nuit. Denoël et Steele, 1932, and Gallimard, 1962
  (Pléiade Edition). Translated by John H. P. Marks as *Journey to the
  End of the Night.* New York, New Directions, 1934, 1960.
(A number of minor texts, not included here, can be found in the Balland
  Oeuvres. A useful bibliography, containing references to various
  articles, speeches, prefaces, and letters, has been published in
  L'Herne, III [1963], 317-27.)

SECONDARY SOURCES

Books

CHESNEAU, ALBERT. *Essai de psychocritique de Louis-Ferdinand Céline.*
  Minard, 1971. Although flawed by use of psychological jargon, this
  book is important for its treatment of Céline's obsession with
  foreigners, outsiders, and "others."
HANREZ, MARC. *Céline.* Gallimard, 1961. Good introduction to Céline.
  Especially strong on Céline's style. Now somewhat dated.
HAYMAN, DAVID. *Louis-Ferdinand Céline.* New York: Columbia
  University Press, 1965. Introductory pamphlet.
HINDUS, MILTON. *The Crippled Giant.* New York: Boar's Head, 1950.
  Recounts the author's personal relationship with Céline in the late
  forties. Still stimulating. Impressively fair-minded.
KNAPP, BETTINA L. *Céline: Man of Hate.* University: University of
  Alabama Press, 1974. Attempt at Jungian analysis of Céline with
  emphasis on his anti-Semitism. Author expresses a strong dislike of
  Céline in a book that seems hastily put together. All too often fac-
  tually unreliable. Good example of an otherwise sane critic and
  serious scholar out to "get" Céline.
MCCARTHY, PATRICK. *Céline.* London: Allen Lane, 1975. Best available
  biography of Céline. Throws fresh light on his whole life and explains

Céline's anti-Semitism as result of deep pessimism, self-hatred, and jealousy of Jews.

MAHÉ, HENRI. *La Brinquebale avec Céline: Cent lettres inédites.* La Table Ronde, 1969. An indispensible view of Céline's private actions and opinions as revealed to a faithful friend.

MORAND, JACQUELINE. *Les Idées politiques de Louis-Ferdinand Céline.* Pichon et Durand-Auzias, 1972. An essential book for comprehension of Céline's political tangles.

OSTROWSKY, ERIKA. *Céline and His Vision.* New York: New York University Press, 1967. Contains many deep insights into Céline's work, but never treats any one work as a whole.

——— *Voyeur Voyant: A Portrait of Louis-Ferdinand Céline.* New York, Random House, 1971. An entertaining biography. Largely outdated by McCarthy book.

POULET, ROBERT. *Mon ami Bardamu: Entretiens familiers avec L.-F. Céline.* Plon, 1971. Originally published in 1958 under slightly different title, this book sympathetically recreates the author's conversations with Céline.

QUÉRIÈRE, YVES DE LA. *Céline et les mots.* Lexington: University of Kentucky Press, 1973. Stylistic study of words and their effects in Céline's work.

ROUX, DOMINIQUE DE. *La Mort de L.-F. Céline.* Christian Bourgeois, 1966. Deeply sympathetic, provocative biography that exonerates Céline of political wrongdoing.

THIHER, ALLEN. *Céline: The Novel as Delirium.* New Brunswick: Rutgers University Press, 1972. Analyzes use of delirium scenes in Céline's work. Sound and useful study, although it omits reference to possible influence of Léon Daudet's *Le Rêve éveillé* on Céline's delirium technique.

VANDROMME, PAUL. *Louis-Ferdinand Céline.* Editions Universitaires, 1963. Book strongly represents the point of view that Céline was not an anti-Semite.

Articles and Reviews

ALMÉRAS, PHILIPEE. "L'Onomastique caricaturale de Louis-Ferdinand Céline." *Revue Internationale d'Onomastique,* XXIV (1971), 161-79. Analyzes Céline's use of proper names.

HINDUS, MILTON. "Louis-Ferdinand Céline: Excerpts from His Letters to Milton Hindus." *Texas Quarterly,* V (1962), 22-38.

——— "Céline: A Reappraisal." *Southern Review,* I (1965), 76-93.

——— "The Recent Revival of Céline: A Consideration." *Mosaic,* VI (1973), 57-66. These articles express grave reservations about Céline as a man, and therefore ultimately about his work. Hindus is always fair.

172 LOUIS-FERDINAND CÉLINE

MAIERHÖFER, FRÄNZI. "Versuch über Louis-Ferdinand Céline." *Hochland,* LXI (1969), 244-57. Links Céline's *Voyage* to development of literature of the absurd.

MAMBRINO, JEAN. "La Petite musique de Céline." *Etudes,* 339 (1973), 219-37. A fine introductory article on Céline's thought and style.

NETTELBECK, COLIN W. "Journey to the End of Art: The Evolution of the Novels of Louis-Ferdinand Céline." *PMLA,* LXXXVII (1972), 80-89. Argues for consideration of Céline's work as an organic whole. As such, it is seen as ultimately expressing a kind of optimism.

———"The Antisemite and the Artist: Céline's Pamphlets and *Guignol's Band.*" *Australian Journal of French Studies,* IX (1972), 180-89. Considers *Guignol's Band* as a great work in which Céline implicitly admits and atones for his prior overt anti-Semitism. Well-written, lucidly argued, but a bit forced.

ROUX, DOMINIQUE DE. *L'Herne,* III (1963) and V (1965). These two full issues of this review are totally devoted to Céline. Acquaintance with the various — and often contradictory — views expressed herein by the many contributors should be the starting point for any serious study of Céline.

SMITH, ANDRÉ. "Céline et la notion de complot." *Etudes Francaises,* VII (1971), 145-61. Analyzes Céline's hostile attitude toward royalty, *bourgeoisie,* clergy, and common people.

THIHER, ALLEN. "Céline and Sartre." *Philological Quarterly,* L (1971), 292 - 305. A good beginning on an important case of literary influence.

Index

DATE DUE

DEMCO 38-297